JUSTITIA

Justitia

Multidisciplinary Readings of the Work of

Jasmin Vardimon Company

Edited by

Paul Johnson

&

Sylwia Dobkowska

First published in the UK in 2016 by Intellect, The Mill, Parnall Road, Fishponds, Bristol, BS16 3JG, UK

First published in the USA in 2016 by Intellect, The University of Chicago Press, 1427 E. 60th Street, Chicago, IL 60637, USA

Series: Playtext
Series editor: Patrick Duggan
Series ISSN: 1754-0933
Cover designer & typesetting: Sylwia Dobkowska
Copy-editor: MPS Technologies
Production manager: Jessica Mitchell

Print ISBN: 978-1-78320-528-8
ePDF ISBN: 978-1-78320-529-5
Printed and bound by Taylor Brothers Bristol

Photographs by Ben Harries on pages: 14, 15, 86, 87, 88, 130, 134
Photographs by Alastair Muir on the cover and on pages: 6, 7, 16, 17, 18, 22, 23, 24, 27, 28, 31, 32, 39, 40, 41, 42, 43, 48, 49, 50, 51, 52, 53, 55, 58, 59, 60, 61, 63, 64, 66, 67, 68, 69, 70, 71, 72, 77, 80, 83, 84, 85, 92, 100, 110, 111, 112, 122, 126, 142, 155, 156, 157, 169, 170

CONTENTS

Performance

Justitia

*Concept, Direction &
Choreography*
Jasmin Vardimon

*Created with
& Performed by*
Paul Blackman
Luke Burrough
Tim Casson
(or David Lloyd)
Christine Gouzelis
Victoria Fox
(or Mafalda Deville)
Athanasia Kanellopoulou
(or Esteban Fourmi)
YunKrung Song
(or Aoi Nakamura)
Jasmin Vardimon

*Associate Director
& Dramaturgy*
Guy Bar-Amotz

Scriptwriter
Rebecca Lenkiewicz

*Costume
& Set Design*
Merle Hensel

Lighting Design
Chahine Yavroyan

*Soundtrack
Design & Edit*
Ohad Fishof

PERFORMANCE

STAGE 2

THE FRONT
COVER

Readings

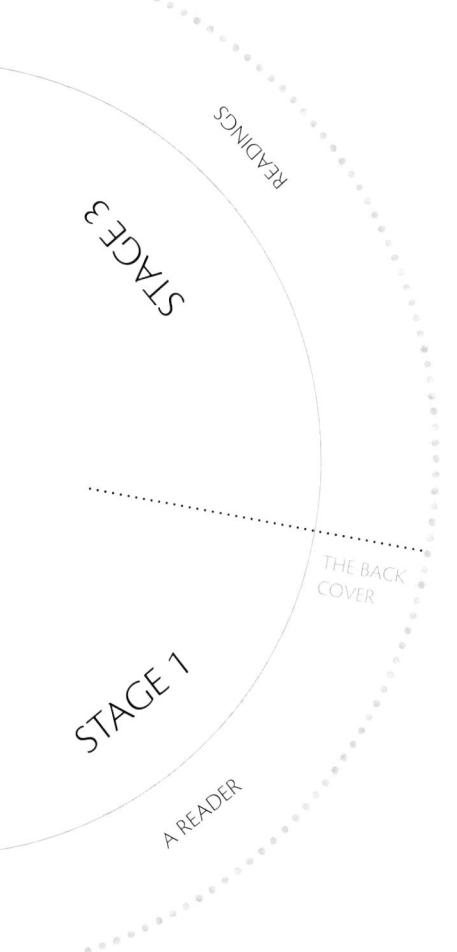

STAGE 3

READINGS

THE BACK COVER

STAGE 1

A READER

ACKNOWLEDGEMENTS

I would like to thank all those who engaged their creative minds in analysing and interpreting *Justitia*: from the creative team and performers who took an active role in interpreting my tasks and directions in the process of creating their parts, to the different performers who relived their roles, and finally to those who created and contributed to this book.

My curiosity to hear these multiple voices and understandings led to this book. The contributions – even if they, in part, contradict or disagree with what I intended – are all relevant and present the individual's perspective.

Some of my initial intentions, metaphors and meanings are still to be discovered and understood, I hope. But here my search for an answer to the question "Does what we see dictate our point of view, or does our point of view dictate what we see?" continues.

Jasmin Vardimon
March 2014

Introduction

Paul Johnson

The work of art comes into being not in the mind of the artist, or on the page, or in the rehearsal room or stage, but in the act of reception, as the mind makes meaning from it. As André Lepecki observes, as "we, the audience, leave the theatre – still energised by the dance that is now no longer present, that is already cooling in our bodies – a fresh new sediment of experience spreads out in our memory, claiming its space as a new past" (1997: 71). This book is an attempt to extend the understanding of a complex, multifocus, multidisciplinary performance through a series of varied responses from a range of different disciplinary and personal perspectives. For Lepecki, "One must pay attention to the spectres in the dance […] because those moments of interruption, of suspension between matter and memory, […] open up doors, slash the narrow boundaries of the descriptive eye, cut the vulgarity of interpretation and description, expand the self into the non-timely real of the room of dancing memories", and so "we write with dancers a shared rehearsal and participate in a dance of intelligence" (1997: 75).

This book grew out of a desire to expand the possibility for the reception of performance to be an inherently creative act. In early 2012, a symposium funded by the Higher Education Academy convened to explore ways of developing collaborations between theatre and dance practitioners and universities. This international and multidisciplinary panel gathered at the Stour Centre, the home of Jasmin Vardimon Company, to view and respond to a studio performance of *Justitia* (2007). The initial invitation read: "We aim to assemble a panel of thinkers and creative minds, with expertise in a wide range of disciplines and invite them to debate, analyse and respond to a specific performance." For Vardimon, the audience's creative response to a piece is a vital extension of the work itself, and a breadth of disciplinary, social and cultural experiences added to the possibilities of those responses. This book attempts to capture the creative response of an audience and tries to find a way of turning that ephemeral experience into something more lasting.

DANCE/PHYSICAL/THEATRE/PERFORMANCE

There is often a difficulty with nomenclature for performance in the genre. Frequently, the term "physical theatre" is used, and, as Sánchez-Colberg observes, "the development of what has been loosely termed 'physical theatre' has marked one of the most significant trends in dance and theatre since the 1980s" (2007: 21). The difficulty with the term, however, is precisely as a result of the significance of that trend, in that the range of performance work described now (by companies, promoters, academics and others) as physical theatre includes such a broad range that the term merely signifies the absence of a realist staging of a play text. Sánchez-Colberg goes on to claim that:

> At a surface level, the term has been collectively used to identify an eclectic production commonly understood to be one which focuses on the unfolding of a narrative through physicalised events and which relegates verbal narrative – if at all present – to a subordinate position. However, it is precisely on evaluating such eclecticism that one is faced with a problem. To admit to the above mentioned generalization would allow us to equate productions as varied as a Christmas pantomime to the work of Grotowski, or, indeed, Bausch. The problems arising from this are obvious.
>
> (2007: 21)

Works by Jasmin Vardimon Company, and others, such as Vincent Dance Theatre and DV8 (increasingly so), often make significant use of text and verbal narrative. Whilst this is seldom in a dominant position, it is certainly not always subordinate to the physical action. Rather, with other performance elements (scenography, music, film, etc.), it is a thread that is woven into the whole. Sánchez-Colberg sets forth a hybrid model of physical theatre that draws on a twin lineage of dance and avant-garde theatre with a focus on the body in space, but this focus on the body runs the risk of reducing the complexity of the performance through a focus on the marker of its difference. With Vardimon's work, in particular, to focus on the body at the expense of the text, narrative, scenography or technology would be to lose sense of the real experience of seeing the work.

Alternatively, it might be possible to imagine a continuum of performance running from dance to theatre, with dance theatre (a form of dance that includes elements of theatre) closer to dance and physical theatre (a form of theatre that works through the body) closer to theatre, but from performance to performance, or from scene to scene, or moment to moment the work might move from one end of the continuum to the other. Consequently, the catch-all term "performance" seems most appropriate; Vardimon refers to herself as a director/choreographer, and to her work as "artwork", and the terms "dance", "theatre" and "performance" appear at similar frequencies in the responses to her work that follow. As Sofia Anastasopoulou observes in her writing on *Justitia*: "Jasmin Vardimon's works belong to this hybrid kind of performance in which the genres lose their importance. Theatre, dance, text and new media make up a colourful mosaic" (2009).

JASMIN VARDIMON COMPANY

Founded in 1997, Jasmin Vardimon Company, under Jasmin Vardimon's artistic direction, has become a key British performance company. They are renowned for Vardimon's theatrical eclecticism; a combination of athleticism, text, technology; and a bringing together of the details of human behaviour with an appreciation of the social significance of performance. The company's repertoire includes *Maze, Freedom, 7734, Yesterday, Justitia, Park, Lullaby, Ticklish, Lure Lure Lure, Tête, Madame Made* and *Therapist*.

Vardimon herself was born and raised on a Kibbutz in central Israel; she joined the Kibbutz Contemporary Dance Company and, in 1995, won the British Council "On the Way to London" Choreography Award. Vardimon has been an Associate Artist at Sadler's Wells since 2006. In 1998 she was an Associate Artist at The Place, and from 1999 to 2005 she was a Yorkshire Dance Partner. She is the recipient of numerous awards including the 2013 International Theatre Institute Award for Excellence in Dance; the Jerwood Choreography Award (2000); the Jerwood Foundation's "Changing Stages" Award (2004); The London Arts Board "New Choreographers" Award (1998); The Kent Culture Award's Artist Award, Destination East Kent Award and Canterbury Award (2014); and the Dimitrije Parlić Award, Serbia's most prestigious award for choreography (2013). Vardimon was a Visiting Professor at the University of Wolverhampton from 2011 to 2013 and received an honorary doctorate from the University of London in July 2014. She developed a postgraduate diploma, at Royal Holloway University London, for dancers and actors, and in 2012 launched JV2, a full-time certificate course at her company's home base in Ashford.

Since its inception, the company has made work that attempts to create meaning for its audience. As Mairead Turner, writing on *Lullaby* (2003), observes, Vardimon's "work illuminates the way that society and its institutions deal with the underbelly of our experiences, instabilities and sicknesses" (2005). *Lullaby* explored sickness, hospitals and the body as a home and as a battleground. As Sanjay Roy observes, the show "hinges on a double vision: illness as alien invader, or as integral to self" (2003). Typically, for the company, this is a piece imbued with athleticism, but athleticism that serves a purpose of generating meaning: focusing attention on the body, and its strengths, weaknesses and desires, and what happens when the body turns on itself.

Part of *Lullaby* was integrated into *Yesterday* (2008), a ten-year retrospective that has been restaged several times. The piece brings together sections from previous works, but with no central narrative; rather, it is meditation on memory, and how memory works on and through the body in various ways. Both of these pieces work through the materialisation and realisation of abstract ideas: "putting metaphors into material form" (Roy, 2008). It is these realisations of abstractions that provide the material from which the audience generate meaning.

Justitia, or Lady Justice, was created by Jasmin Vardimon Company in 2006, and premiered in 2007. Its narrative focuses on a death, a court case and a confession, with the audience, initially at least, placed in the position of the jury. The set (designed by Merle Hensel), a revolve that covers the whole stage, is divided into three locations: the courtroom, the crime scene and a group therapy room. As the revolve turns clockwise and anticlockwise, it moves time forward and backward, shows new perspectives, and gives new understandings. The court is a place where the attempt is made to produce a concrete conclusion from a series of potentially contradictory viewpoints: to generate meaning as either guilty or not guilty. The audience do not ever get an easy resolution; not only are multiple possibilities presented but a tidy denouement is avoided.

This book then is an attempt to record what it was like to experience *Justitia*, and to give the reader a richer, more nuanced understanding than a video recording, or a description, or a review, or a single academic analysis can give. Whilst there are methods for precisely recording movement, such as Labanotation, this book is instead interested in a phenomenological exploration of a performance event: contradictory and varied as that may well be. There are times where the reading of the text may be at odds with what is presented in the script, or in the video recording, but we have deliberately left those contradictions in place.

There are a number of different *Justitias* referred to in this book: the original performance in 2007; the studio staging for the symposium in 2012; the restaging in 2013; and the recording on DVD. None of these is privileged as the authentic performance, and the authors of this book have their experience of the piece shaped by which of those they saw, and when.

In this series of responses we also avoid presenting the definitive interpretation: the correct answers are not at the back of the book. The intention is that this is a book that performs, rather than a book that dissects a performance. Instead, it provides visual and textual interpretations, and the intention is for the different sections of the book to speak to each other. An illustrated script gives a sense of the performance for those who have not seen it, and a recording of the work is available from the company. This is followed by a series of responses developed from the symposium, where respondents were originally required to give their initial reaction the morning following the performance. Nina Stieger discusses collaboration and creation, and what *Justitia* is really about as opposed to what merely happens in it. Emily Kasriel explores agency in the piece, and the difficulty of reading this, and how it is performed. For Noam Segal, time is the central way of understanding *Justitia*, while Libby Worth explores how juries, and audiences, come to conclusions. Felix Ensslin gives a philosophical first response, weaving together revenge and the responsibility of witnesses, while Christine Harmar-Brown responds as a writer. Paul Brill gives a lawyer's perspective on the representation of a court case, and the texture and mess that is involved. Amanda Stuart Fisher develops the idea of the confession, and what remains when a performance is gone. Finally, Royona Mitra compares watching devised performance with the work of a jury.

Various moments of the piece are returned to; various themes are explored from different perspectives. These multiple, and often contradictory responses give the work a new life beyond the auditorium, a "moment of revisiting and restaging the dance in the scene of writing and the scene of memory" (Lepecki, 1996: 71). The final piece, by Geoffrey Colman, returns the circle: from response to a performance to the work in the rehearsal room prior to performance. Again, this is not to privilege the "insider-position", but to reflect the ongoing nature of process, performance and response, and the meaning that is generated at all of those stages.

CREDITS

ANONYMOUS WRITER
(performed by Jasmin Vardimon)

CASSANDRA
(performed by Christine Gouzelis)

CHARLIE CAIN
(performed by Luke Burrough)

MIMI KIM / MRS CAIN
(performed by YunKrung Song / Aoi Nakamura)

SETH MARVELL
(performed by Paul Blackman)

JB / TJ
(performed by Tim Casson / David Lloyd)

VERONICA HUNT
(performed by Victoria Fox / Mafalda Deville)

MISS CARESY
(performed by Athanasia Kanellopoulou / Esteban Fourmi)

STAGE 2 *Justitia*

PART ONE

PART ONE

(Outdoor space: JASMIN types)

(Courtroom: CASSANDRA takes over typing)

(MIMI, CHARLIE in Courtroom: Carpet duet)

(SLOWLY TYPED TEXT ON SCREEN)

Charles Cain and Mimi Kim met in 2004 in Hong Kong.
That year Private Charles Cain's garrison was deployed to Brunei.
Miss Kim was in her second year of studying anaesthesiology in Hong Kong.
Weather conditions destroyed a local school near to her university. Kim volunteered and taught the children in the open air. Private Cain spent his leave helping to rebuild the classrooms. They met and formed a close friendship amidst the debris.

A month later they flew off together to Italy. They visited Pompeii. And it was there in the ruins, where time had stood still for centuries, that Private Cain asked Miss Kim to be his wife. He promised to look after her. He wished that they could petrify into a shape together like the twisted volcanic eternal figures that surrounded them. They were married. Private Cain retired from the military and became a security guard. Mimi Cain is in the last year of her medical studies.

(CAIN's front room. CHARLIE CAIN and SETH MARVELL: Sofa duet)

(In the back garden. CHARLIE, SETH and TJ: Soldiers unison)

(CAIN's front room. CHARLIE and SETH run and sit down to watch the football)

SETH:	Well, turn the game on!
CHARLIE:	Alright, I'm putting it on. Still ten minutes to go. Could go to extra time.
SETH:	I've been waiting to see it all day.
CHARLIE:	Well, there you go.
SETH:	Yes, we're in the lead.
CHARLIE:	Come on boys about time we had a decent result.
SETH:	We're going to win the league this year!
CHARLIE:	Shhh! Shhhh! Alright Marvell, don't get carried away. Remember what happened last season, you had to put that stupid bet on.
SETH:	I didn't put that bet on, you put it on.
CHARLIE:	I'm no betting man Marvell; you know that.

(Outdoor space: JASMIN typing)

JB: All rise.

(Reprise)

(VERONICA HUNT addresses the audience as the jury)

VERONICA: My lord, ladies, gentlemen of the jury, the defendant stands accused of murder. On the evening of the 27th of September, my client Mrs Cain was at home with her husband Mr Charlie Cain, and the deceased, Mr Seth Marvell, who was often a visitor to their home. On the night in question, all three were consuming alcoholic beverages and watching television. Mr Cain left the house at around twenty past nine to replenish supplies. He returned at half past nine to find Mr Marvell dead through a fatal head injury. What happened in those ten minutes that led to his unfortunate death?

Ten minutes, six hundred seconds. Infinite moments. Endless events may happen to each one of you in that same precise pocket of time. During our short recess later on, you may meet a former lover in the lobby by chance. Perhaps you run to the shop to buy a newspaper. You fail to see a black cab coming round the corner. Your world is changed forever. Ten minutes is both a finite world of recorded time and an infinity of possibilities. You might reconcile with an enemy in that time. Fall in love. Take your own life. Nothing is certain.

We might believe that tracing the events from twenty past nine to half past nine of the said night is a simple chronological map. But from another viewpoint, it is a myriad of questions and open-ended mystery.

What is certain is that if we could replay those ten minutes moment by moment, blow by blow, my client would walk away from these proceedings a free woman.

(Courtroom: All rise)

JB: All rise.

(Reprise)

(VERONICA HUNT addresses the audience as the jury)

VERONICA: My lord, ladies, gentlemen of the jury, the defendant stands accused of murder. On the evening of the 27th of September, my client Mrs Cain was at home with her husband Mr Charlie Cain, and the deceased, Mr Seth Marvell, who was often a visitor to their home. On the night in question, all three were consuming alcoholic beverages and watching television. Mr Cain left the house at around twenty past nine to replenish supplies. He returned at half past nine to find Mr Marvell dead through a fatal head injury. What happened in those ten minutes that led to his unfortunate death?

Ten minutes, six hundred seconds. Infinite moments. Endless events may happen to each one of you in that same precise pocket of time. During our short recess later on, you may meet a former lover in the lobby by chance. Perhaps you run to the shop to buy a newspaper. You fail to see a black cab coming round the corner. Your world is changed forever. Ten minutes is both a finite world of recorded time and an infinity of possibilities. You might reconcile with an enemy in that time. Fall in love. Take your own life. Nothing is certain.

We might believe that tracing the events from twenty past nine to half past nine of the said night is a simple chronological map. But from another viewpoint, it is a myriad of questions and open-ended mystery.

What is certain is that if we could replay those ten minutes moment by moment, blow by blow, my client would walk away from these proceedings a free woman.

(CAIN's front room. MIMI lays down the rug.
CHARLIE and SETH walk in to watch the football)

SETH: Well, turn the game on!

CHARLIE: I'm putting it on. Still got ten minutes to go yet. Could
             go to extra time.

SETH: I've been waiting to see it all day.

CHARLIE: Well, there you go.

SETH: Yes, we're in the lead.

CHARLIE: Come on boys about time we had a decent result.

SETH: We're going to win the league this year!

CHARLIE: Shhh! Shhhh! Alright Marvell, don't get carried away.

SETH: (sings) We're going to win the league … We're going to
             win the league.

(MIMI strikes SETH)

VERONICA: Objection! I would like to remind the prosecution that we are at the beginning of an inquiry and not at the end and what has been inferred is both prejudicial and inflammatory to the case.

If we could only replay those ten minutes we would have indelible proof that my client is not guilty of murder.

VERONICA: Objection! I would like to remind the prosecution that we are at the beginning of an inquiry and not at the end and what has been inferred is both prejudicial and inflammatory to the case.

If we could only replay those ten minutes we would have indelible proof that my client is not guilty of murder.

(CHARLIE and SETH rewind and leave the room, then re-enter)

SETH: Well, turn the game on!

CHARLIE: I'm putting it on. Still got ten minutes to go yet. Could
             go to extra time.

SETH: I've been waiting to see it all day.

CHARLIE: Well, there you go.

SETH: Yes, we're in the lead.

CHARLIE: Come on boys about time we had a decent result.

SETH: We're going to win the league this year!

CHARLIE: Not yet Marvell, don't get carried away.

(MIMI enters)

MIMI: Hi Marvell. Hi Charlie.

CHARLIE: Hello darling, Seth's just here to watch the game; there's
             only ten minutes to go … you don't mind, do you?

SETH: Hey Mimi, how are you doing?

(SETH and MIMI touch hands while MIMI embraces CHARLIE)

VERONICA: Objection! There is no evidence to suggest that my client and Mr Marvell were involved in anything more than a platonic relationship. Nor that they had any significant contact with each other outside of the friendship enjoyed by them and Mr Cain.

(MIMI sits between SETH and CHARLIE. MIMI acts as if she is on speed)

(MIMI sits between SETH and CHARLIE. MIMI acts as if she is on speed)

VERONICA: Objection! The suggestion that my client was "high" or indeed drunk is inaccurate. No traces of amphetamine or other illegal substances were found in her system. There was a low alcohol count found present in her blood. This was a result of social drinking on the said night.

VERONICA: Objection! The suggestion that my client was "high" or indeed drunk is inaccurate. No traces of amphetamine or other illegal substances were found in her system. There was a low alcohol count found present in her blood. This was a result of social drinking on the said night.

(CHARLIE and MIMI are on the couch. SETH joins them.
He brings a bottle of whiskey in)

SETH: Surprise. I brought you a present. Me!

CHARLIE: Fantastic.

SETH: No. It's actually a bottle of Bourbon. A token of appre-
             ciation from one of my patients who's just left therapy.
             Guess what, he says he is never coming back.

CHARLIE: I bet they all say that, don't they Marvell.

SETH: Nice one, Charlie.

(SETH disappears behind the sofa and returns with glasses)

SETH: Well, we're going to need some glasses; well, let's get cosy.

CHARLIE: Ladies first.

SETH: Speaking of ladies, Mimi you look absolutely wonderful.
             Can I say something Charlie, married life suits you.
             It really does.

CHARLIE: I'll drink to that. Cheers!

MIMI: Cheers!

SETH: Cheers!

(CHARLIE and MIMI are on the couch. SETH joins them.
He brings a bottle of whiskey in)

SETH: Surprise. I brought you a present. Me!

CHARLIE: Fantastic.

SETH: No. It's actually a bottle of Bourbon. A token of appre-
                ciation from one of my patients who's just left therapy.
                Guess what, he says he is never coming back.

CHARLIE: I bet they all say that, don't they Marvell.

SETH: Nice one, Charlie.

(SETH disappears behind the sofa and returns with glasses)

SETH: Well, we're going to need some glasses; well, let's get cosy.

CHARLIE: Ladies first.

SETH: Speaking of ladies, Mimi you look absolutely wonderful.
                Can I say something Charlie, married life suits you.
                It really does.

CHARLIE: I'll drink to that. Cheers!

MIMI: Cheers!

SETH: Cheers!

(They have a drinking sequence)
(CHARLIE then excuses himself)

CHARLIE: I'm not drinking that all night; I've got work in the
            morning. I'm going to get some beers; can I get you any-
            thing? I'm only going up the road to Majjo's. I'll be back
            in ten minutes.

MIMI: Okay.

SETH: Well, you take your time.

CHARLIE: And you take care of her …!

(CHARLIE exits. MIMI and SETH kiss. CHARLIE looks for his keys)

CHARLIE: Mimi, have you seen my wallet? … Oh no you're fine. It's
            that pocket again. See you!

MIMI: Bye!

SETH: Bye!

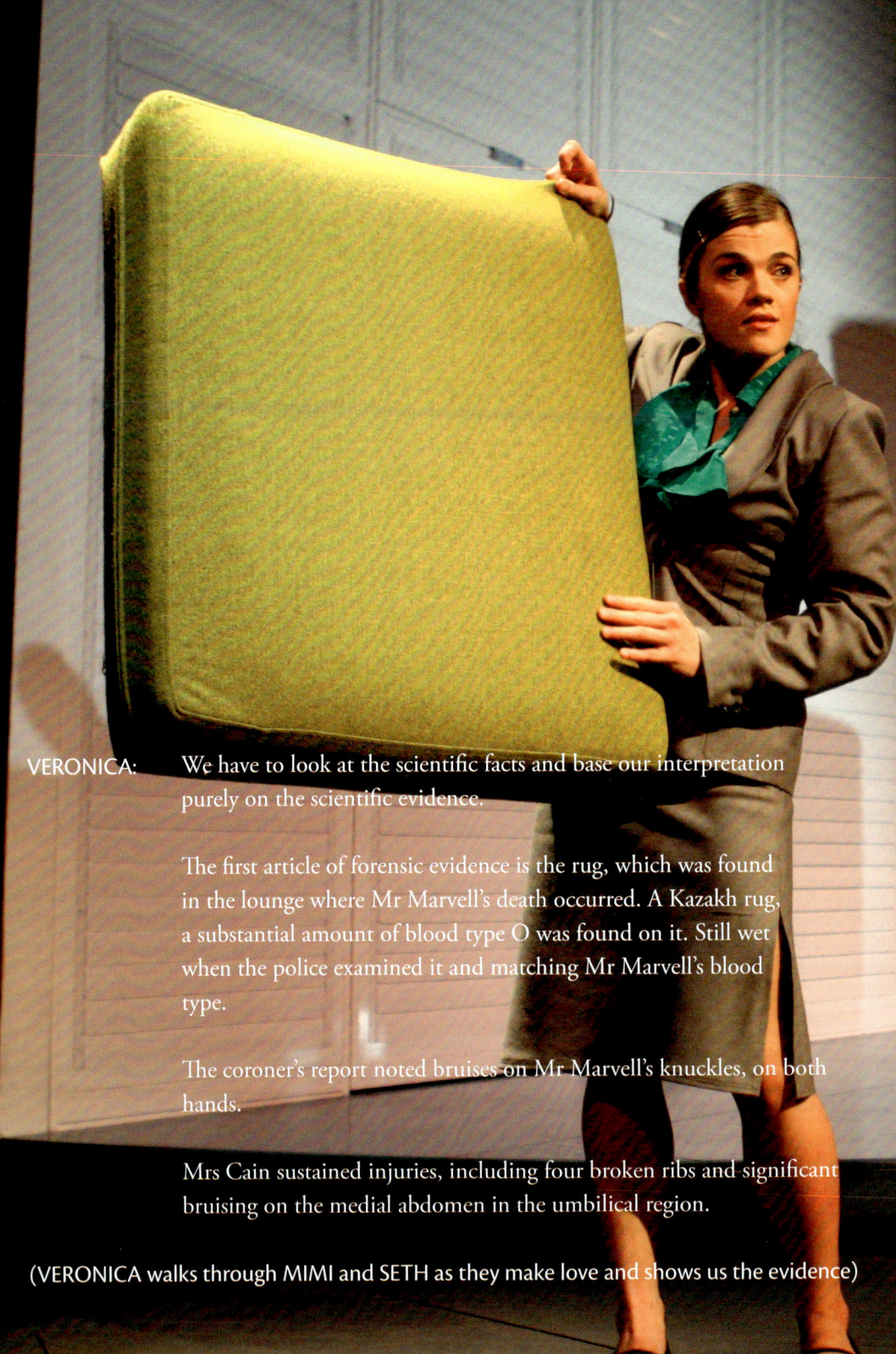

VERONICA: We have to look at the scientific facts and base our interpretation purely on the scientific evidence.

The first article of forensic evidence is the rug, which was found in the lounge where Mr Marvell's death occurred. A Kazakh rug, a substantial amount of blood type O was found on it. Still wet when the police examined it and matching Mr Marvell's blood type.

The coroner's report noted bruises on Mr Marvell's knuckles, on both hands.

Mrs Cain sustained injuries, including four broken ribs and significant bruising on the medial abdomen in the umbilical region.

(VERONICA walks through MIMI and SETH as they make love and shows us the evidence)

Mr Marvell's shirt was stained with blood, again type O. A bloodstain that appears to be the result of pooling blood and gravitational runoff. My client's fingerprints were found all across the shirt.

Fresh semen was found in the fibres of the settee. It was found to be Mr Marvell's.

Mr Marvell sustained a major blow to the head, which damaged his frontal lobes. It seems like a heavy object came into contact with his head and crushed a small area of his skull, which resulted in haemorrhaging and subsequently death.

Mrs Cain's hair was found on both the arms and the padded seating area of the settee, a partial clump of hair rather than strands suggesting a struggle.

Particles of skin were found under Mrs Cain's fingernails that matched with the DNA of Mr Marvell.

(CHARLIE returns and finds MIMI on the couch and SETH on the floor)

VERONICA:

ion! There   to

stantiate this   Wh

have just witnessed

supposition.

intent on

submitting

(The scene rewinds)

to ion! There

Wh stantiate this

have just witnessed

supposition.

intent on

submitting

(The scene rewinds)

Object   is nothing

sub   theory.   at

you   is all

                The prosecution

seems   omitting fact

and   fiction.

(The Therapy Group enter. SETH MARVELL arrives. First group therapy)

SETH: So. Welcome. Welcome to the group. I am Seth Marvell and I will be leading you in these group therapy sessions. What you all signed up for, and what connects each of you to each other, is a disproportionate feeling of guilt. So what we're going to try and do today is break the back of that burden of people living with guilt.

So, who wants to start?

The belief that you have done something wrong, this is what causes guilt. This is a result of you judging yourself or the feeling that someone else is judging you.

Is this how you feel?

CHARLIE: No.

SETH: How can we live without guilt? What if we simply abolish the concept of guilt. But if we do this, what happens to conscience?

CHARLIE: Sorry?

SETH: What about social boundaries?
            (To Charlie) Look how about starting today?
            How about starting with your name?

There is a word we use for people who live without guilt. Someone who is not constrained by what harm their actions may cause to others. We call them sociopaths. Any sociopaths here today? No?

Good, then let's get the ball rolling …

TJ: Alright, my name is TJ, and I'm here today because my dad has paid for me to be here. He says I can't use his car unless I come to these sessions.

SETH: Guilt can immobilise. It is one of the worst feelings a human being can experience. So what is guilt? It's a religious concept. But it is also a fundamental issue in psychotherapy within the psychodynamic tradition. In other words, or put more simply, it ties you up in knots, makes you feel unworthy and pretty miserable.

When are we ever free of guilt? It's a biblical belief that Adam was naked and guilt free in the Garden. He was innocent. As innocent as Walt Disney's Bambi. Neither Adam nor this cartoon character could ever be accused of being worthy of guilt. But we're talking fantasies here. Eden and Bambi's forests have been replaced by cities and corporations, where no one can really achieve their mythical purity and should not feel guilty for leading a less than snow white life.

CASSANDRA: Hi. My name is Cassandra. And I'm here because I'm guilty. I am guilty of making other people guilty. I studied stenography for two years. And now … I write people's lives. I sit in court and my transcripts decide on their fate. And I'm fast. Real fast. So fast that lives just flit by. Whatever verdict they are given is determined by what I write. If I wrote something different down they would be able to walk out of the court. Free.

SETH: Now that's a good start.

(The group clap and move in a line and out of the therapy room)

(MISS CARESY gets lost and ends up in CHARLIE's kitchen. Neighbour visit: MISS CARESY and CHARLIE)

VERONICA: The plaintiff's main witness is the Cains' next-door neighbour.
             She claims to have witnessed the events of that night.

             The notion of neighbour has always been important throughout history.
             The Bible tells us to "Love your neighbour as yourself". The lawyer in
             the Bible replies, "But who is my neighbour?" A question that I reiterate
             in reference to Miss Caresy. No further questions.

                        (The courtroom. JB and CASSANDRA)

             (Security guard sequence. CASSANDRA climbs down the walls and types)

                                (VERONICA enters)

VERONICA: Mr Cain is a very protective husband, some would say over protective.
             I would venture further and state that once he had Mrs Cain on British
             turf he became in fact very controlling, territorial and manipulative in
             his behaviour towards his wife. Instead of asking her to do things, he
             would order them to be done. You can take the man out of the military,
             but you can't take the military out of the man.

                        (MIMI and CHARLIE enter. Control duet)

             (VERONICA and CHARLIE, with CASSANDRA and SETH dancing in the room behind.
                                    Unison duets)

             (The men finish up holding the women up against the walls)

                        (JB holds MISS CARESY against the wall)

                  (CASSANDRA and VERONICA climb down the wall)

(Discredit scene. VERONICA assaults and gets rid of MISS CARESY.
CASSANDRA types. TJ watches)

VERONICA: I should like to question the witness. Miss Caresy?

My Lord. Ladies. Gentlemen. Gentle. Men. The witness claims to be a
hard-working member of our society.

I am going to wind you, all of you, around my shapely finger. I will lead
you to decisions you never dreamed of by the tip of my manicured nail.
The blade of my stiletto will slide against your throats, cold, steel, invit-
ing, terrifying.

This woman has taken money from the mouths of young children by
carrying on indiscriminately with their various fathers. Young Freddy
may not receive his first bike this Christmas because his father spent the
money on this woman instead. Perhaps Freddy will never learn to ride a
bike. He will lead a life of social isolation in both park and playground
because this woman could not stop herself from doing her very own
cycling in the sweaty saddle.

Are you sorry? For getting in my way? I walk on people. Did you know
a stiletto is actually a type of knife? If I cut you, do you bleed? Come
here. I'm sorry. No. Actually, I'm not. And you don't smell like a virgin
should smell.

I put it to you that her statement is not just unreliable but fabricated.
Whether this web of fabrication is conscious or confused is irrelevant. It
holds no weight against the reputation of the accused.

Thank you.

(CAIN's front room. The rape scene)

(MIMI strikes SETH)

(VERONICA rolls up the rug)

(MISS CARESY and JB dance. CASSANDRA, VERONICA, SETH, CHARLIE and MIMI
join in the courtroom. End of Part One sequence)

VERONICA: I put it to you now, the jury, to deliberate and decide. A woman's life, her future is in your hands.

Do you believe my client to be guilty of murder in the first degree? Or do you judge that it was manslaughter? Or indeed that Mrs Cain was acting in self-defence?

The court will adjourn for a short recess.
We will reconvene in twenty minutes.

(Kung Fu sequence)

PART TWO

(MISS CARESY enters. Confused witness)

(CASSANDRA and VERONICA HUNT enter. CASSANDRA types)

VERONICA: I have presented every conceivable aspect of the night that the attack took place. Without prejudice, but with a supreme will to out the truth.

MISS CARESY: No! You haven't dealt with the only story that doesn't ever make sense. The love story. Where you fight until you don't recognise your own face. There is no logic in the battle. Just pure emotion. Where is this one? "El crime del passion".

(MIMI's front room. The crime of passion version. MIMI and SETH)

SETH: For Christ's sake, stop it. Do you think that's sexy? Look at yourself. Put your clothes back on. Just because a woman's naked doesn't mean a man wants her, you know?

Did you never hear of the word restraint? Or you probably don't have it in your language?

I wonder what Charlie would say? You think this is what he imagined when you said "I do"?

(MIMI strikes him)

(The courtroom. CASSANDRA types. MISS CARESY and VERONICA.
Floor arms sequence)

(JASMIN types and CASSANDRA dances. The typist solo)

(TYPED)

I type therefore I am. I am therefore I type. I type type typo. Typo. Erratum.
Sometimes I imagine that the people who I write about are attached to the keys.
Through an invisible spider thread that I weave around them. Their lives are dictated by
the electric ink on the screen. When my fingers get tired, my mind catches fire. I think
about things while I type. People. Things I shouldn't think about. I never made mistakes
before. Typos. I still don't actually make mistakes on the page. But in my mind. There are
blots and typos everywhere. Therapist. The rapist. No. Wrong spacing. Therapist. He was
a good man. But I killed his healing. By loving the healer, I killed the cure. It's my fault.
My fingers' fault. I typed faster than they could speak. I transcribed his death. With
the tips of my fingers.

(SETH and JB enter. CASSANDRA and SETH climb the walls.
JB sets up a microphone)

(VERONICA enters. MIMI and CHARLIE sit)

VERONICA: The Kazakh rug can tell us a story about what happened that night.
               In Ancient Persia spies would leak information out of and into the
               country through a code that was hidden in the pictures and the figures
               of their finely woven carpets. What message would Mrs Cain's Kazakh
               rug convey to us if it could? It could tell us the whole story as simply
               as one unfolds a carpet.

(SETH enters. Microphone duet. SETH and CHARLIE)

(CASSANDRA watches from the walls)

SETH: Good evening … I'm going to share a little story with you; I'm going to tell you how I, Seth Marvell, ended up dead on the floor?

It's very strange when the cord snaps. The communication cord. … and that's exactly what happened.

So. There I was on the couch with his wife. And I said to her …

Look, truth is important. Don't you want to hear what happened that night? Or are you all stuck here like I am?

So there I was, and I said to her something she just did not want to hear, but it was her response …

Her response was so passionate. … I just had to do it.

CHARLIE: Do what Seth? What did you have to do?

SETH: He would like to know ladies and gentlemen.

CHARLIE: If the police arrest you, everyone assumes, instantly, that you're guilty. They do. They did. My wife is innocent. Do you hear me? Pure!

TJ: Excuse me Sir, the court is closed for the day.

(CHARLIE is taken out by JB)

(MIMI's front room. MIMI. Sofa solo)

(VERONICA's bedroom. CASSANDRA and SETH on the walls. VERONICA. Mattress solo)

(CASSANDRA through the various rooms following SETH. Following scene)

(Revolving sequence
of different lives.
Ending with MIMI and
VERONICA in their rooms,
VERONICA practising
her speech)

VERONICA: The first article is the rug.
                My Lord.
                My Lord, the first article
                I would like to show you is …
                is …
                is the rug.
                The rug.

(The group therapy room. CASSANDRA and SETH. Chairs duet)

(Group therapy members enter. Second group therapy)

SETH: So. Welcome back to this week's group therapy session. It's great
          to see you are all here again. Together. Because that is what it's all
          about. Being together.
          So what we're going to do today is just jump right back in and take
          the bull by the horns.

                    (SETH lifts MISS CARESY)

          Ok everyone. Let's give her some support.

                    (MISS CARESY stands and says nothing)

          That's fine. We're not in a hurry. As long as you feel … supported.
          But, sometimes all you need is a push in the right direction. So up
          you get TJ. Just say sometime, whatever is on your chest just say
          something, just say something …. You guilty bastard.

                    (SETH pushes TJ into the arena)

TJ: Alright, my name is TJ. I like it. I like the feel of it in my hand. Just
          stroking it. Knowing it's there. Ready to shoot. My gun. The trigger.
          It makes me feel … here. Like I can do anything. Anyone. It makes
          me feel, makes me feel. Hard.

MISS CARESY: Hard!

TJ: What are you laughing at, Suvlaki?

                    (MISS CARESY and TJ encounter each other)

SETH: Now, that's great. That's what I like to see, a bit of group involvement. A bit of group interaction.

          So, well done, TJ.

          It's not easy getting up and saying a few words about yourself, is it, but there we are.

          We conquered a mountain. Who's next to climb?

VERONICA: Hi. My name is Veronica and I'm here because I …. I ….

                    (The group move)

          Hello again. My name is Veronica. Veronica Hunt.
          I'm thirty four.

CHARLIE: I'm thirty four. I've no brothers or sisters … and I'm not in
          a relationship. …. Ah and you live in Streatham!

VERONICA: I'm thirty four. I've no brothers or sisters. And I'm not in a relationship.
          I'm not quite sure why I'm here. In this group I mean, not generally.
          I'm not very good at the whole talking thing. I mean I can talk. And
          I cope with stress very well. Pretty well. But lately I keep getting
          stuck.

          I am here because I …. I ….

I live in Streatham. Which is fine …. I like these sessions. I like driving. I like that feeling of covering distances. You get in your car and you know where you have to get to and you get there. I like it, getting from A to B. But I don't like it as much as I used to. I'm a good driver. I take bends very smoothly. I like the motorways. At night. All you can see of the other cars are tiny lights. Red and white. I like the anonymity of it. But I haven't been on a motorway for a long time. I killed someone. A child. Her name was Lisa. She was three and a half. Three and a half or three and a quarter? I ran her over. In my car. I'd just bought it. A vintage red spider sports car. The roof comes down. And I hit her. In the early morning. She ran out into the road. I was sober. I wasn't speeding. A child in the road at six in the morning isn't my responsibility.

She had been a flower girl at a wedding the night before and she was so tired when her dad put her to bed that he left her in her bridesmaid's dress. She walked out into the middle of the road. In her white dress. I was turning a corner, not fast, but not slow because it was so quiet everywhere. It was all tree-lined residential streets, no lights on in houses. Only the orange of street lamps. I was listening to a talk show. And suddenly I saw her. Stood there. Like an angel. Just looking at me. I wasn't going fast but you just don't expect to see anyone out at that time. It was almost like a dream for a moment. Like I'd imagined her. I remember thinking she looked a bit like me, like I looked at that age. Puzzled expression. I'll never forget her expression. I braked. Really, really hard. And I bit my tongue. But there was this noise I'll never forget. Of her hitting the car. It wasn't loud. Just very … real.

I turned the car off and got out. I couldn't see her body. I didn't know whether I should get back in the car and drive on a few yards to free her or if that might do more damage. Although actually I knew. Stood on the pavement. I knew that driving forward or backward would make no difference. Because I'd seen. Even in that one moment. How small she was. Very small. And it was very still under the car. I stood on the pavement with my arms crossed. Silent. And her mother ran out next to me. Who was silent too. For a moment. Then her mother made a sound. Like she had asthma. And then she threw herself onto the concrete pavement and went under the car and she was breathing loud like she was asthmatic and she kept saying "Shh shh shh" to her daughter. Who was dead.

I visited her mother weeks after it happened. The kitchen was full of paintings that Lisa had done at nursery. A bear. A princess. A butterfly. A blue bird.

I would like to be as light as a butterfly. I would like to have wings instead of legs. Sometimes I can't feel my legs. Or my arms. Or my head. Sometimes I feel funny. If it's hot outside I feel cold instead. If I go swimming I can't feel the water. I was walking through the park the other day with my mum and I looked up at the sky and I turned round and round and round. But when I stopped turning, the earth was still standing still. It wasn't going round like it used to.

(Outdoor space; JASMIN solo)

(MIMI in courtroom and sits. Confession scene)

(Group enter)

(JASMIN types script in English on screen while MIMI speaks in Korean)

MIMI: I'm here because I'm guilty .... guilty of saving a life.
        I studied medicine. Anaesthesiology. The art of numbing pain. And
        yet after years of studying how to prevent it I inflicted the pain.
        Fatal pain.

        Seth threatened to take my baby away from me. Telling me to mur-
        der the baby like it was nothing. A problem. Just an obstacle.
        He said I must get rid of it. That Charlie would know it was not
        his. Could not be his. I didn't care. What is marriage? Friendship?
        Hurting someone's feelings compared to this feeling of creating life
        inside of me? When I knew I was pregnant it was the first time I felt
        complete. Strong. Stronger than I imagined was possible.

        Animals protect their young. And that's how I feel more than ever
        before. Animal. Except animals don't feel guilt.

        Opposite our flat is a prison where the last woman in the UK was
        hanged. Fifty years ago. 1955. I saw a picture of her. She was my
        age, twenty-eight. While she was pregnant her lover attacked her.
        She miscarried after he punched her in the stomach.
        I took a life to save a life. Save my baby's life.

        Is that what you wanted to hear?

        And what if I am lying?

(Outdoor space: JASMIN solo)

(MIMI in courtroom and sits. Confession scene)

(Group enter)

(JASMIN types script in English on screen while MIMI speaks in Korean)

MIMI: I'm here because I'm guilty .... guilty of saving a life.
I studied medicine. Anaesthesiology. The art of numbing pain. And yet after years of studying how to prevent it I inflicted the pain. Fatal pain.

Seth threatened to take my baby away from me. Telling me to murder the baby like it was nothing. A problem. Just an obstacle.
He said I must get rid of it. That Charlie would know it was not his. Could not be his. I didn't care. What is marriage? Friendship? Hurting someone's feelings compared to this feeling of creating life inside of me? When I knew I was pregnant it was the first time I felt complete. Strong. Stronger than I imagined was possible.

Animals protect their young. And that's how I feel more than ever before. Animal. Except animals don't feel guilt.

Opposite our flat is a prison where the last woman in the UK was hanged. Fifty years ago, 1955. I saw a picture of her. She was my age, twenty eight. While she was pregnant her lover attacked her. She miscarried after he punched her in the stomach.
I took a life to save a life. Save my baby's life.

Is that what you wanted to hear?

And what if I am lying?

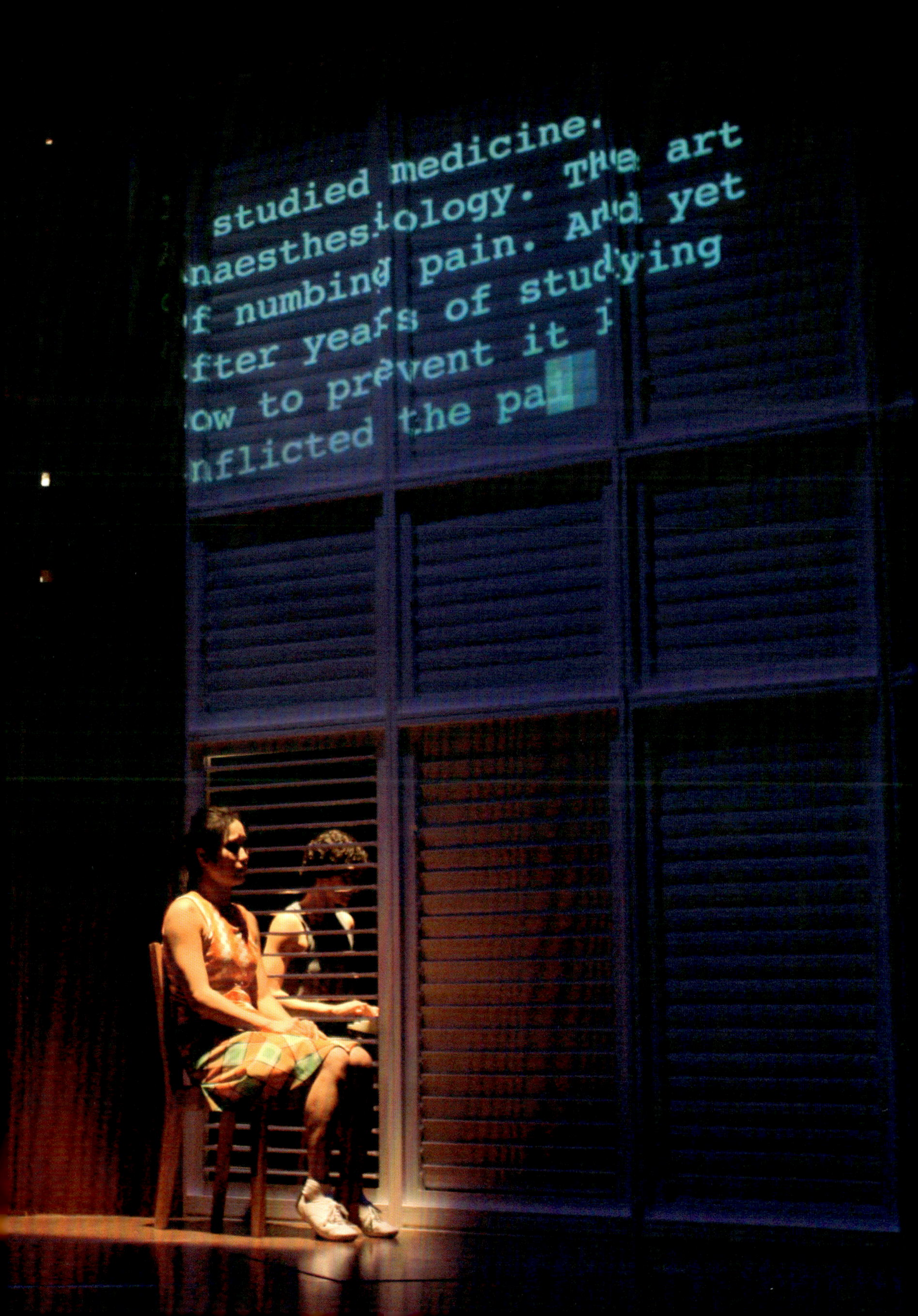
studied medicine.
naesthesiology. The art
f numbing pain. And yet
fter years of studying
ow to prevent it i
nflicted the pa

(Revolving sequence)

STAGE 3
Readings

Analysis and Creation

Nina Stieger

In the past twenty years of my work with writers, I have revisited a few questions over and over again. Where do ideas come from? When does the act of creativity begin? How is it that there are so many different kinds of artists and approaches to text? What is the artists' "voice"? How can we be sure our audience sees in our work what we intend to communicate or provoke? In all my years of asking these questions, it occurs to me now that the deepest challenge to the artist is to continue refreshing their view on the world and to continue sharing their vision in fresh ways, maintaining their voice but finding new ways of expression.

I worked with Jasmin Vardimon on her piece, *7734*, in 2010. Through this process, I discovered her to be a "writer" of extraordinary vision, able to see a truly visual piece of work as a text and to imagine its story, months before it had been made. In our first meeting, we had coffee and she tried to tell me what she thought the show might be like, ideas and emotions it would capture and explore. I specifically recall the fact that our meeting took place in a café at Euston Station because she was leaving to perform another piece and was still very much inhabiting the "other world" of this project. That project was *Justitia* of course; I often think of this reality for the working artist – simultaneous projects mean one project is delivered while the next is in its inception – as a "marinade". I marvelled at her ability to put words to what were, in some ways, a series of inchoate ideas. We both said how hard it was to describe something as yet unformed and also to assign specific meanings to abstractions and those early whispers of inspirations.

Although this is common practice in my work with playwrights, I found working with "choreographer as author" different in many ways. Throughout the collaboration, I found that particular task the most difficult and the most exciting; that is, to extract "story" from gestures, expressions and choreography, and then to shape, trim and enhance this story through dramaturgical and structural narrative techniques. And to speak – or write – it through with Vardimon: this was the part of our process that was most intimate and could be most awkward. I'd sit in on a rehearsal, try to map the emerging structure of the two acts, scene by scene, and then, that evening, send a long e-mail to Vardimon, essentially conveying what I saw, what it meant to me and what I felt it meant to the piece as a whole. But without dialogue or plot points, it was a complex parsing process to identify what elements carried which story beats, and I usually tried to find a balance between the abstraction that gives great art its power and the specificity that allows it to connect with the heart of the individual. For me and Vardimon, the words risked getting in the way, and I hoped we could speak the same language. The left brain and the right brain had to find a way to communicate.

Vardimon is always interested in how people "read" and analyse her work. She says that interpretation is an extension of the artwork and that she values the perspective of various people's "lenses". We are asked for our reflections on *Justitia*. I'm not sure if I can extend as much as reflect, with distortions, blind spots and strange ways of seeing.

The first thing is to try and articulate an important distinction between *what happens in this story* and *what this story is about*.

What *happens* in this story? A writer writes. A murder is tried. A lawyer dies.

The meat of *Justitia* is not really there though.

What is this story *about*? The difference between transcription and invention. The fallibility of memory and the impossibility of discerning the truth. The complicated ways we identify with each other through empathy, proximity and intimacy.

And it's also really deeply about the subconscious. The piece dramatises the conflicting impulses to explore, to gratify and to suppress this living part of ourselves and it puts this almighty struggle on stage, with the subconscious posited as the seat of truth. What kind of truth does the subconscious hold? We sublimate impulses that embarrass us. We bury our deepest secrets beyond the reaches of our awareness. Pressing towards pathology, our fears can express themselves as phobias; our desires as fetishes. Our subconscious holds a treasure trove of prejudices, atavistic urges and self-deceptions. But some part of psychology holds that, really, we just want the truth to come out. We want to be seen, shamed, even punished if necessary, but seen.

In *Justitia*, the components all suggest the desire – need, even – for the truth to come out with a cathartic imperative. For instance, the set reinforces this idea with its pocked, peep-holed and slatted walls – borders that invite you to peer through into the next room. Restless stirrings rattle the chairs. Whatever's in there can't be hidden – or hidden *from*.

The "cross-dressed neighbour", Miss Caresy, is the perfect symbol of the slipperiness of truth. Sure, she was a witness, but we can't trust her any more than we can trust our own eyes looking at her. Witnesses are unreliable, and so are our own impressions and memories, to say nothing of our desires. How do I know what I've seen? What do I really want? In fact, how do we know anything? *Justitia* slides us through the key-holes that separate sex and rape, murder and self-defence, the accidental killing of a child and the simple failure to protect it. How do we ever know what really happened? What IS reasonable doubt? Does the attribution in intent determine how we are judged?

Did we see the same things in the recurrent gestures in *Justitia*? To me, the stenographer typed like a seamstress. I saw Cassandra poised like a watchful spider in the upper corner of the room and saw her hands move like they were spinning webs and weaving interpretation into facts. I kept seeing hands moving almost like rudders, or sometimes like an oar. It made me think of the characters as being guided by strong internal forces, sometimes morality, sometimes impulse.

I saw a lot of movement when knees were locked, awkwardly pressed together and then powerfully pulled apart. I saw this as the physical effort to keep things in, battling against the stronger desire to let them out. There was another repeated movement, often done en masse, almost tribally, when one hand would brace the elbow of the opposite arm, and it looked like things were welling up and spilling over, like a rush of truth washing over each person like a ritual bath.

Finally, there was the motif where one person would "make another" move in a certain way, a kind of puppetry of power, or human-scale ventriloquism. This last is particularly interesting for its connection to the subconscious. When the ventriloquist's dummy speaks, whose thoughts and desires does he express? When Marvell and Mimi are puppeted in battle, whose desires are reflected?

So the truth wants to come out. But what's true? Life and death are true. The story of Ruth Ellis is true. Her first words at the scene of her crime were "I am guilty. I'm a little confused". What Vardimon said about analysis extending the work has made me think of something else. How many iterations of analysis can a piece like this sustain? When does analysis give way to creation? As "lenses", are we reliable witnesses?

And, with that in mind: Who is *Justitia* – Lady Justice – anyway? The stenographer? Cassandra? The lawyer? Jasmin Vardimon? Me?

I often find the process of working on scripts one of luck, timing and instinct. The most crucial part is often the alchemy of writer, director and cast. Then there is

the big bang of the play itself connecting with the world. The process of working with Vardimon, and indeed, of seeing and trying to grapple with a piece of *Justitia* feels even more about the kismet of bringing together units of meaning to create impressions, and, eventually, a story. What I have developed a greater sense of is the communion she insists upon through the audience, who bring their impressions, biases, prejudices, fetishes and subtext. From out of dark emerges a dynamic conversation between "writer" and "world" about what we see, how we know, things we feel. Perhaps, the encounter allows artist and audience to inhabit the imagined world together, both involved in a simultaneous leap of creativity. It brings to mind the following quotation from GB Shaw: "Imagination is the beginning of creation. You imagine what you desire, you will what you imagine and at last you create what you will."

The Idea of Agency in the Performance of *Justitia*

Emily Kasriel

Each performance of *Justitia* is a dynamic, highly textured event that draws upon a vocabulary of movement, speech, recorded sound and music, projected text, lights, narrative and testimony. The interplay between these different complex strands creates plentiful opportunities for new combinations and interpretations. There are many ways the performance can be read. Ambiguous interpretations and multiple readings fold neatly with the central narrative of *Justitia*: overlaid and contradictory readings of a central narrative event – a murder. A central question that can be asked of this complex performance is who holds power, the choreographer, dancers or the audience?

The idea of agency has a rich and multi-layered meaning and I am going to use agency as a tool with which to explore *Justitia*. Agency is a theme that suffuses the work, but in a manner that is constantly shifting and at times appears ungraspable. Even the cast themselves may not always be aware of where the agency lies within each performance. For the audience, a reading of agency is even more fluid.

I am going to consider an agent as a person who is the subject of an action, who has the capacity to choose between options and is able to do what she or he chooses. An agent may act individually without recourse to others, but I will also consider the possibility of joint agency. In a further interpretation of agency, the philosopher Immanuel Kant developed a theory that incorporated the exercise of autonomy. He believed that because we are all autonomous, each of us requires a social space within which we can freely determine our own actions (Schneewind, 1992: 310).

Dance theatre is a rich genre through which to consider the idea of agency because of the ambiguity embedded in a live performance. The audience is not watching a film or reading a book, but instead watching dancers creating an event in front of them, in the moment. The performance will never be precisely the same twice. On each occasion the dancers have the power to improvise and to act on impulse. There is the possibility of chance movement, and also failure to achieve a desired movement or spoken outcome. The audience, witness to the performance for the first time, is not always able to differentiate which movements are those directed by the choreographer and which are spontaneous and unique, performed in a certain way on this occasion only.

At the start of the performance, we become witnesses to a stenographer typing in a purposeful focused manner. We are not told whose ideas she is writing down, but her mechanical movements give the impression that they are not hers, as there is no evidence of deliberation or thought. The letters and words are flowing through her arms and through her fingers onto the keys of the typewriter, as a stream of liquid passes through a siphon, with no apparent agency. However, soon the stenographer seeks to assert herself. We see an interruption in the tight mechanical gestures. It is as if, from within her self, she has awakened and begins to interrupt this flow of information from ear to hand. Initially with just one arm, she begins to mediate the flow with an increasing poetic urgency. Soon her whole body is erect and expressive. It seems that the authority that determines what the stenographer has to transcribe, a scientific positivist force, is being mediated by her more visceral, emotional, less structured self, so that her ideas can now flourish and she is able to embellish the original text. As the performance unfolds, the individualised movements assume a greater degree of strength, with her animated dark shadow enlarged and projected onto the set behind her. The creativity of her ideas is echoed by the balletic, flowing movements that increasingly take hold of her left side. We are witnessing a struggle for authority and for control, with the woman's body the contested battleground. The dutiful work that she was initially carrying out, and which she continues to execute, becomes increasingly altered and personalised by the increasing passion that unfolds before us. It is as if the original ideas are now being given the freedom to be explored and expressed in a more powerful and authentic manner.

The motif of words and movements vying to be the medium through which control is exerted runs throughout the performance. At one point one of the stenographers types "I type therefore I am, I am therefore I type". We are unsure which medium is privileged, which medium drives the narrative; the words or the dance. In many of the scenes the stenographers are present, typing, but whether they are directing the action or merely recording or decoding it is left unclear.

While movement appears to be an indication of agency, for this to hold true, the movement needs to be attributed to the agent herself. In the performance of *Justitia*, there are a number of instances when this appears not to be the case; the movements themselves suggest that intentionality is absent. While the performers may be in motion, they do not appear to be in control of their movements; they are not in a relationship of authority with their own bodies. Near the start of the piece, Charles Cain and his new wife Mimi emerge from an open door like dolls out of a Swiss cuckoo clock, moving in small, stilted, regular steps, shuffling along, as if a plank underneath their feet is projecting them forward. At the start of this scene, they are only able to move in unison, the blanket acting as a plank beneath their feet excludes the possibility of individual momentum. Their status as newly-weds is projected on a wall, documented or directed by a stenographer sitting unobserved in the corner of the stage. At the very start, the stenographer introduces them as Charles Cain and Mimi; by giving the man's full name, while his wife is only given a first name, which is itself a diminutive one, a power relationship is already created between the couple. The carpet under their feet, which had appeared to control their movements, now assumes a new function, as Mimi "chooses" to begin to wrap herself inside it before Charles takes the lead, wrapping and engulfing her. Mimi then continues to move doll-like while Charles is able to assume control over her, pick her up and move her across the stage and out the door, becoming the primary agent in their relationship.

The following scene, in which Charles Cain and Seth Marvell loaf about and play fight on the sofa, involves a dynamic interpretation of agency. The music is confident, even aggressive. Both characters are acting in a way that projects an assertion of power and control: control over their own bodies and control over the space that surrounds them. Charles and Seth occupy the physical space with confidence; they battle to seize the TV remote as they fight to control each other. The movement of the male bodies appears exaggerated with an unreal intensity. Conversely, their machismo movements also suggest an inner vulnerability as they vie to assume dominance over the sofa; it becomes apparent that they are unable to control other aspects of their lives.

When they are removed from the domesticity of the sofa scene and transferred seamlessly to a new setting, they are initially supreme in their physical prowess. However, as the scene unfolds, and the music becomes less melodic and more threatening, with shouts added as the environment slowly transforms into a theatre of war, the men seem to be transformed into victims. Though they are still acting as fighters with a masculine confidence and strength, they are no longer in control. Their bodily movements become more jerky and reactive. Their choices become more limited as they begin to retreat, fearful for their lives. At times we are unsure of the line between their play fighting and real war. It is purposefully blurred, as we are not certain whether the war is an ever-present memory or a reality still being played out.

In one of the versions of the night of the murder, which is played out as events rewind, Mimi is drunk, exuberant and controls the scene. In another Mimi, Charles and Seth act together, drunk, as a single unified agent. Through the different scenes, Charles and Seth compete for Mimi's affection, with Mimi herself playing the role of seducer or seduced. In some of the versions of events, Mimi acts impulsively and uses a tool, the oversized lamp, to exert control over the situation, and Seth is killed. Through the different scenarios, the two men are able to use their bodies as force fields. Their agency is their strength. When we see the scenario played out in which Mimi is a seductress, she too uses her body, but because of her relative weakness, she can't overpower the men. As her advances are rejected, she appears naked, desperate, foolish and vulnerable. Though she is in her own home, a setting in which we may aspire to be at ease, comfortable, relaxed, she appears ill at ease and on edge and diminished. Increasingly, she seems unable to occupy the space with confidence, as if she has no right to be there. It is as if the space has been conquered by a male physicality, leaving no room for her female form to express itself on its own terms. In Kant's terms, Mimi is deprived of the ability to assert her own agency.

In many parts of the performance, the dancers are acting as a unified collective force, appearing to be controlled by a single external agency as their movements echo each other. In the scene in which the defendants, lawyers, police authority and lawyer move along a series of chairs, they permit themselves no individual personalised expressions. Though they laugh, an expression of personal emotion, all the characters laugh together in a forced jolted manner, as their heads tilt towards the same direction; thus minimising their individual agency. The chairs beneath them seem to dictate their roles, which they are all forced to comply with, along with the barked repeated orders. "All rise". As the scene progresses, it is almost as if the characters are able to assume an agency together, a genuinely unified agent, rather than a differentiated group of characters controlled by another outside power.

In another scene, Mimi and Seth play out a fight like Kung Fu characters. The music is frenetic and driven, and the movements of both characters are fast and aggressive. They appear to parody action heroes from a comic book setting. Yet just behind them, but still clearly visible to us, are dancers who are dressed in black hoodies and tracksuits. It is these anonymous black-costumed stage hands who are controlling the two characters. They lift and move Mimi and Seth, giving them the semblance of autonomous action, while simultaneously controlling them like puppets.

Throughout the performance, Veronica, the Defence Lawyer, attempts to be the overriding power, struggling to assert control over the outcome of the trial, and of the future life of her defendant Mimi, by telling us *her* story of the events on the night of the murder. Veronica wishes to influence the way that we as audience, as jurors, perceive the story; we see her attempting to control the whole narrative of the performance. The tool of her authority is the spoken word, articulate and forceful. She pleads her case at the same time as the dancers play out the drama. At times they appear to be illustrating the truth as Veronica sees it, but in others their actions are in direct contradiction to her version of events. The audience is thus led to perceive her as an unreliable narrator. At times Veronica overwhelms us because her words are spoken with such a degree of emotional intensity, which sweeps her up as she becomes breathless. It is ironic that the increasing intensity and personalisation of her argument lessen the power to convince us. In an environment like a court of law, the greater the passion, the more sceptical we may feel as a witness or member of the jury that Veronica is speaking the truth.

In another scene, we see Veronica in the intimacy of her bedroom, unable to sleep as she goes over the details of the case. Deprived of her professional attire, we see her as vulnerable; she is wearing her pyjamas. Veronica no longer projects the appearance of control. Yet ironically, in this exposed situation, she appears to have greater agency than during her orator performances. It is as if the facts of the case, which she projects with so much force in other scenes, control her. In contrast, in this bedroom scene she challenges the facts, wrestles with them, and in doing so reveals her humanity and her power.

In the reoccurring "group therapy sessions", Seth Marvell is dressed in a silver waistcoat as he assumes the role of an entertainer, a real performer. He is empowered by the possession of a microphone that he uses to control whose voice gets heard. At first glance he is the ultimate agent here, asserting what in a therapy session would be an inappropriate degree of control and humiliation. He tries to force the private to become public. He attempts to exert control over his clients and pull their guilt like reluctant rotten teeth from their bodies, so that everyone can share gleefully in the pickings. Their guilt is his gold. If they confess, he is enriched. Unlike a therapist, Marvell is not interested in his clients being empowered and healing themselves, though the words he uses parody this role. Instead, Seth seeks to control his clients so that they are disempowered; the clapping that he encourages when a member has confessed their guilt becomes aggressive bullying, which we witness as shouts and intimidating actions. It is as if the private demons of the confessor are personified by the group: harrowing, blaming, threatening and hounding the victim.

However, everything is transformed when Veronica decides to confess. After an introduction about the joys of driving, in which she is unable to hold the attention of the group and they appear bored, she is able to assume agency over the room through her compelling narrative. Suddenly her group stops dozing and wakes up. We don't know if the story is true or woven, though the emotional intensity enables her to control the group and us as the audience. In her story she is the agent, the one who killed the child dressed in white, who appears as Jesus the innocent. The child has no agency, as she is too young to have any role in or responsibility for her own death. In the story, though the child ran out onto the road at 6am, it feels as if the child was carried there; it is as if fate or indeed Veronica herself had, without wanting to, assumed agency over the child to compel her to walk into the road. As a viewer I am obliged to witness this intimate confession, and the poignancy of the story and the emotional intensity of the music compel me to respond, invoking feelings of terror and sorrow. I wait for someone who is beyond the narrative, who is ultimately in control of which scenes are played, to spin the set, rotate the room and transform the scene being portrayed, so that I am able to escape the feelings of artificial sorrow manufactured by the story of the girl's fate.

While we are aware throughout the performance of the creative agency of the choreographer Jasmin Vardimon, we as audience have become increasingly drawn into the performance, into the drama of the various characters. As we become immersed in the narrative, we are seduced into the illusion that the dancers and actors are moving and speaking with their own agency. The spinning of the set reminds us that there is a greater agency at work in the performance. The choreographer doesn't only have a vital power, being able to change the setting for the action by literally spinning the set, but as an auteur she also determines the movement and voice of the dancers and actors. Though her direction has been interpreted by them, it is her intentions they realise on stage. On some level, creativity is the ultimate act of agency. The creative power of the choreographer invokes not only the capacity of choice, of acting (or thinking) according to her will, but also the power to act or get others to act according to her self-consciously chosen rules. When the choreographer is creating a work of dance, she is autonomous. While she may choose to borrow from certain genres and other pieces of dance or dramatic work, she has a high degree of freedom in the world that she can create and realise. The highly prioritised place of movement within the performance gives scope for a very fluid narrative in which words or movement can carry the story, leaving a lot of scope for ambiguity and multiple readings. In so far as the audience "judge" the performance they witness on stage, the fluidity means that there is little that is right or wrong. The choreographer acts as an agent in creating her own rules, but has a further degree of control; she is able to break any laws that she has created for herself.

Throughout the performance, much is made of the stenographer, and other performers struggle for agency through the medium of the circular rotating set. At some moments in the performance, the individual dancers run through the different environments, struggling to assert control over their own lives and actions as the rooms rotate with increasing speed, placing them quite literally in situations not of their choosing. At times they are trapped, frozen by the change of scene, thwarted in their attempts to express their desires, to move as they choose. On other occasions, some of the dancers attempt to get back to where they wanted to be. They do this through opening doors, crossing over boundaries between these scenes, either by obeying the "rules" of the set and walking through doors, or occasionally by transgressing the rules by walking outside the walls or even, very shockingly, by rolling over the top of the walls of the set. Here the dancers transform themselves from being human characters who obey gravity and norms of walking on the ground, to becoming animal-like and free, prowling up other dimensions to escape, attack or hide. In one of the final scenes, the walls themselves assert their agency over all of the characters, who are deprived of their capacity to move, act or speak, to type or think. The dancers become mere dolls strung up to dry by the force of the set, their bodies all placed similarly at a diagonal. They are no longer individuals as they have become devoid of passion and expression. They no longer have identities. They have become merely the vessels into which the story has been poured and expressed. They are all equal; equally powerless before the set, the director, and ultimately before us, who have the ultimate agency to decide on our interpretation of who is guilty and innocent, and moreover whether we are convinced by the validity of the performance itself.

"Owl of Minerva": the mythical bird, a sacred symbol of Minerva, the Goddess of Wisdom.

Representations of Time in the Performance *Justitia*

Noam Segal

In this chapter I will discuss the various perceptions of time and historical approaches as represented in Jasmin Vardimon's performance *Justitia*. Vardimon confronts different historical concepts through theatrical and narrative tools. Their use in a criminal trial highlights the legal and moral consequences of the conceptions and draws the viewer into a historical and ethical discussion.

A BRIEF HISTORY OF TIME

The classical civilisations of Greece and Rome were ahistorical. According to their understanding, history had no specific direction, that is it was neither linear nor did it embody historical significance. Furthermore, history did not include any assumptions about the end of time or the end of days.

It was Christianity that developed a new sophisticated and ambiguous attitude to time; it acknowledged both cyclical and chronological time; it outlined the difference between life and afterlife and gave meaning to each one of these frameworks, as explained by Oskar Cullmann in his book *Christ and time* (1964). Judaism exchanged a periodical understanding of time for a chronological perspective that gives every stage of life, including the afterlife – as perceived by devout and Messianic Judaism – meaning. Similarly, Christianity could only give history a purpose and direction by voluntarily giving up its secular sense, as the fulfilment of history is the end of history. Thus, Aurelius Augustinus has divided history into six stages, which will come to an end on the seventh course: the end of the world.

In the Renaissance, the concept of historical consciousness developed further and the time that had been hostile and destructive became friendly by rejecting the obsession with the end of days and exchanged it with a yearning for utopia. This was the time when history became understood as a science studying progress, changes in time and the relations between civilisations, for example as Lord Acton defined history in his prologue for *The Cambridge Modern History* as "progressive science". Modern history was developed by the rationalists during the Enlightenment. By secularising the Renaissance, rationality was restored to the historical process. History was seen as a continuous process of progress toward the perfection of the human condition. The cult of progress culminated during the Enlightenment.

The religious idea of the "end of history" also pervaded secular historical thought and led to the principle of the end of history, which clarifies the penetration of religious thought into secular history. Scientists from various disciplines believed modern history was the last phase of humanity as it incorporates clear signs of the end days. Marx also assumed that the proletarian revolution and the cancellation of social classes meant the end of history; Daniel Bell declared the end of Ideology in the 1960s; Francis Fukuyama talked about the end of civilisations in his acclaimed book from 1992 *The End of History and the Last Man*; Bill Mckibben announced the end of nature in 1989 and Charles Berlitz had stated in 1999 that the end of time was just around the corner. In general, the end of a century, or the end of a millennia, has always led to the emergence of various apocalyptic beliefs: the end of ideology, the end of history, etc. During the twentieth century, sociologists, philosophers and artists had a measurable impact on the concept of historical time. The discussion no longer revolved around the end of time, but rather around the multiplicity of social times, fragmentation and innovative reading of time units.

Every concept of time, whether religious or secular, modern or primitive, entails a moral system. The concept of linear time was adopted by the monotheistic religions and enabled the establishment of a moral system of punishment and reward. Such moral conceptions served rulers to control civilians. Furthermore, they established a system of values relating to individuals in society even before the establishment of national rules. In a timeless world, our actions would be deleted; there would be no historical memory, collective scars or guilt.

Several primitive societies in the Pacific and south and central America live with a spiral concept of time, whereby each year a ceremony is held in which all actions, statuses and memories are erased; each year they turn a new leaf, start anew Tabula Rasa. Once this ceremony was adopted by the establishment, a value system was established accordingly: a perception that advocates forgetting and turning over a new leaf, while erasing past penalties and providing new opportunities. A by-product of such a system may be an increase in crime levels while contrarily creating greater individual freedom and open and dynamic personalities. However, even when Plato spoke of the ideal state he tried to preserve the belief in celestial punishment and reward – though he himself did not believe in the Gods – as this belief was useful for the purposes of law enforcement. The Enlightenment raised the banner of the discussion about the concept of linear and progressive time, a discussion that had many ethical and cultural implications. Consequently, even a concept of time that favours fragmentation holds various moral implications.

The differences between the various concepts can be found in the questions about time regarding life after death, e.g. messianic perceptions that believe in rewards after death such as hell and heaven or the coming of the messiah. Perceptions of an eye for an eye pertain to a certain time in this life yet can also continue into the afterlife. The Buddhist concept of time reviews events in light of karma and lasting consequences that shift between each reincarnation. Contrarily, existentialism championed the here and now, life itself and denied the possibility of an afterlife. This is a linear concept of time with a limited end point that focuses on life.

STARTING POINT

A typist is typing away on a keyboard in repetitive, circular hand movements. Her circular, spiralling hand movements interlock as they put the narrative into motion on the keyboard. We can already witness a circular motion that occurs while writing a linear narrative with a beginning, middle and end. These contradictions will occur throughout the performance, circular and linear movement, unitary and fragmented time, progression and a spiralling experience.

While reading the text in the background, written by the typist dancer, the audience notices a couple in the centre of the circular stage, moving in circles to the rhythm of the music. The audience slowly notices that the cyclic structure of the stage functions as a space for a number of situations in different locations. One part of the circular stage is a living room that is the crime scene, another part is another living room that is the courtroom, and the third part is an intermediate space that will contain a variety of situations, among them the therapy sessions room. The dancers rotate the stage, create the crossing of segments and narratives, the spaces and the various time segments. Each move from one space to the next is the beginning of a new time segment. As viewers, we see the transitions between one linear narrative (which is the trial that runs throughout the performance between the different sections) and another group of events (which are segments from the group session and re-enactment of various scenes that may or may not have occurred at the scene of the murder). The scenes, including the re-enactments, occur simultaneously on stage, as if to invoke an event that happened rather than consciously re-enacting the scene.

ACT 1

The jurors are seated on chairs while the defence presents its case. While the lawyer argues her case, the characters draw circles with their feet. Once she has finished arguing her case, the lawyer suggests moving in time, as going back in time will acquit her client. The stage rotates clockwise according to linear time, in the direction of time as it functions in our daily lives, back to the crime scene.

The scene is displayed, and stops with each "objection" raised by the prosecution. In this case the dancers "rewind" and trace back their movements, creating a sequel to the scene, according to the claims of the prosecution. In the next scene we see two dancers moving in circular motions on the floor, arranging chairs in a circle and then beginning a session of group therapy led by the deceased, whose death is under investigation in the trial.

At this point, we can mark two timelines and a narrative taking place in the performance. The first is the trial, entrusted with and complying with the system of rational laws. This system operates according to a set of rules and occurs along a linear timeline. According to the rules of the genre, the timeline contains plot developments, and a turning point that leads to an end point after which the plot is resolved and the audience will experience the awaited catharsis. This timeline develops chronologically throughout the play, and is based on the moral principles of the concept of time as associated with monotheistic religions advocating the existence of God. The moral principles upon which this concept is based are present in the performance as they are enacted by the characters. Moreover, this perception of time – morality – takes shape on stage in the clockwise movements and in the choreography displayed as the typist types her text. Writing, which symbolises wisdom and the documenting of history, adds an additional layer of rationalism to this axis of time.

GROUP THERAPY

The dancers gather in one space for group therapy. The deceased, the facilitator, states that the subject of the session is guilt. In fact, he clarifies; the session will deal with a disproportionate sense of guilt. The goal of treatment is defined as the ability to learn to live with guilt, by either ignoring it or incorporating it. He explains that the feeling that you have done something bad causes the sense of guilt and this is perhaps due to the way you judge yourself or someone else's judgement of you.

He sees guilt as a religious concept, a fundamental issue that is part of the psycho-dynamic tradition, and that leads to feelings of worthlessness and misery. This is a religious belief that man in heaven felt guilty for feeling free, "as free as Bambi was in Disney's story", as Marvell cynically suggests. This highlights the impossibility in the concept of freedom. According to him, we are all subjected to a prewritten narrative that negates our freedom. Freedom is a fantasy, he explains, an imaginary cultural construct. Following his line of thought, as no one is really free, no one should feel any guilt.

A woman begins to speak; her name is Cassandra. She describes the sense of guilt that she deals with. Her job entails writing and transcribing people's destinies. Cassandra writes the court protocols. She is present in the courthouse, writes quickly and forges endings. Each word that is inadvertently changed can alter a destiny, distinguish life from death, freedom or slavery.

Cassandra serves just slightly as the "Owl of Minerva": the mythical bird, a sacred symbol of Minerva, the Goddess of Wisdom. Only a smart observer like the owl, who knows the laws according to which history unfolds, who has become sceptical about delicate people's good intentions, can understand the strategic decisions made by prime ministers, great rabbis, magicians of intelligence and bureaucrats, all of whom are enslaved to the illusion of absolute certainty. These decision makers come to conclusions based on "track record", interpret current strategic situations in ways that "guarantee" security and the future, stability and long-lasting peace. Moreover, these decision makers act impulsively; they are prisoners of a fatal obsession, a bias or predetermined decree, and therefore lead to the undesired effect of self-destruction. Cassandra is aware of both these pathologies and functions as one who has the power to change them, unwittingly, by making typing errors, through her profound knowledge of the laws of time and narrative, fate and its arbitrariness.

The group moves around the circular stage in somersaults, as it continues to cross the various designated spaces that stretch along the circular stage.

The second axis that will take place throughout the performance is the pragmatic concept of time axis, seen in the show, with an indeterminate point in chronological time. It exists mainly in the sessions of group therapy led by the deceased. First of all, the deceased, whose death is at the heart of the trial, returns to life to guide the therapeutic sessions, detached from the narrative that is being discussed in the trial that unifies the performance. In his appearance as the leader of the group session, he rejects the linear axis of the performance and of justice. Consequently, the joint participation of the actors and dancers alike, independent of how they function in the performance, provides the viewer with a type of departure point into another dimension of time, which gives a different perspective to the performance. Meanwhile, the deceased does not wait and offers yet another perspective on the trial. In his eyes, guilt is a social feeling imbedded in our souls, the nature of which is an illusion or a mirage. The feeling does not exist objectively, and we need to learn how to talk about it and evade it. He criticises Adam and Eve in paradise for their sense of guilt, and portrays this as a misrepresentation, as deception that is meant to plant the conscientiousness feeling in our hearts. He wants to reveal the control mechanism that the sense of guilt enables and asks the patients to be aware of the manipulation exerted on them. Just like Nietzsche's desire to be relieved of the sense of guilt and historical memory in order to become more Dionysian, the deceased asks the people in the session to release their social restraints and allow their desire to move them. This request assumes that there is no concept of punishment and reward, or no retribution in the afterlife. Everything is here and now.

THE GIRL NEXT-DOOR

After a stormy and sexy dance, the lawyer enters and explains to viewers the importance of the "neighbour" concept. This discussion is accompanied by suspicion that one of the characters had an extramarital affair with the neighbour; that is, there is an accusation of adultery. The lawyer lingers on this term and its religious significance and decides to quote the biblical verse: "Love thy neighbour". Thus, she emphasises the compatibility between the religious sanctions and the legal system – the same compatibility that the deceased indicated during the group discussion, though he was critical of it, and she is not. The lawyer uses the religious imperative to justify the arguments and places religion as a system upon which actions and laws rest. We once again return to the linear perspective of time and to the prosecution's arguments in the trial. This perception of time is accompanied by justifications and religious, legal and social imperatives.

The rest of the trial accompanies the typist who writes or rewrites the prosecution's claim. We see the hand that types, which accounts for acts and sets destinies in stone, in which guilt and time are engraved and temporary or unfinished tales are validated by their inscription into the Papyrus of time. The typist is presented again as an angel of history, whose writing motivates the narrative actions.

RECONCILIATION

In the second part Cassandra breaks into a spellbound dance (towards the audience) in light of the text that is being written behind her, which explains her terrible sense of guilt. As a historiographer of destinies, she becomes a sort of god to the people whose destiny she writes. She explains how a spelling mistake can be a life or death sentence. She turns her back to the future and explores and dissolves into her past. Her past established these people's present. This is a modern concept of time. Throughout history, the modern people turned their backs to the future and examined their past, from which they drew conclusions about the future. Yet they didn't dare direct an independent gaze towards their future. It has been argued that now, for the first time in the history of mankind, we are directing a brave gaze towards the future, and turning our backs to the past.

According to Walter Benjamin's essay "Theses on the Philosophy of History", the angel that appears in the painting *Angelus Novus* by Paul Klee seems to be drawing back from the thing upon which it is looking. His eyes and his mouth are open wide and his wings are spread out to the sides. This is what the angel of history has to look like: he has turned his back on the past. What seems to us as a chain of events appears to the angel as a single catastrophe; one that continuously piles ruins on top of each other and then throws them at his feet. He would like to linger for a moment, to bring back the dead and to mend that which is broken. But a storm that blows from heaven is tangled up in his wings. The winds are so strong that he can no longer bend his wings. The winds of the storm steadily push him into the future, to which he turns his back, as the piles of rubble before him tower to the sky. This thing that we call progress is the winds of this storm. Cassandra seems to contain this dualism: on the one hand, her spirit is hardened as she straightens her gaze towards the historical collective, all along grasping the rules according to which modern time is used. On the other hand, she takes part in this game and wallows in her individual guilt.

In the next scene we see Cassandra hovering like an owl in the lawyer's bedroom. The stage rotates again in a clockwise direction and Cassandra moves in a anticlockwise direction among the other hovering performers. Only her movements go against linear time, while the dancers move the stage. We are exposed to the heroes in all the different spaces, who reveal empty time, a time of introspection and solitude. The stage continues to move in a circular motion to the sound of the lawyer's chatter as she prepares her speech. Time passes as the time of progress, as chronological time, while we are forced into another session of group therapy, detached from time, led by the deceased – a guilt session.

He begins by saying he is "glad to see you all here together, that's all that matters", the "togetherness". The importance of "togetherness" in this life functioned in monotheistic religions as a more secular element that was meant to bring people together and build a community. However, this secular means was not typical of these religions and was in fact contrary to the concepts of reward and retribution that judged the individual and dealt with personal self-examination.

The deceased encourages those present to get rid of the bad, the daily and the transitory elements within them, expressing a wish to return to a prior consciousness in which it was possible to shake off the past, to profess the present and to live according to Sisyphus. At this moment it seems that everyone is having fun, jumping from one time to another, from one situation to another, in a state of consistent formatting. Yet the fun ends abruptly when one woman chooses to ruin the celebration and confesses to killing a little girl in a car accident. Suddenly, all the participants disclaim the hedonistic trance they were in and show extreme discomfort, restlessness and a deep annoyance, which are at odds with the Dionysian atmosphere that existed only a moment earlier. The woman continues to tell the story of what happened and slowly her voice changes to the voice of a little girl, her body language become childish and she gradually becomes a little girl. The stage does not move. Time moves slowly, as it does in difficult moments in real life; no one goes anywhere, they are all stuck in a difficult and real situation from which they cannot escape.

The woman's choice to become the girl that was killed is an ethical choice. At this moment Vardimon chooses sides and exposes her identification with the pain of those whose voice is unheard. In fact, it puts an end to the philosophical discussion by placing the pain of someone absent before those who are present; everyone, the dancers and the audience, takes part in the little girl's grief. This is not a reproach but rather the creation of identification with the suffering of others and a ratification of the sense of guilt as an existing, objective and natural phenomenon. Furthermore, the public exposure has an empowering effect on solidarity. All of us together ("is the only thing that matters", as the deceased said at the start of the current guilt session) take part in the exposure and the pain. As a result, the experience of guilt and pain become more valid, more real and more significant. But they are validated by secularisation, by the ratification and shared experience of the authentic sentiment, not by a dependency on external reasons that originate from religion or rationale.

In the last section we are thrown into a confessional, in which the defendant confesses her actions. She compares different values and justifies the value of the unborn child. As it turns out, the father wanted to abort the baby, and this desire created a game of 'an eye for an eye, a life for a life'; a game of punishment and reward, without which many believe man would not be able to stick to a moral system. Under this principle, the heroine decided to take the life of the baby's father. "I took a life to give a life". The mystery is solved. The morality of linear time and historical guilt wins.

The stage rotates and we see the culprits and suspects scattered around the vast stage, passing by in a anticlockwise direction, frozen in various poses, reconstructing fragments from situations that lead to different parts of the story. Just like the moment before we die, everything flashes before our eyes in a fragmented and a linear motion that counters the direction of daily time. The overview, the final examination, like the final moment before death, turns out to be a sentimental and impulsive moment rather than something rational and linear.

Ringing True

Libby Worth

By chance, in the course of three months, I was invited/required to sit on two jury panels. The first was to respond to a live production of the dance-theatre performance *Justitia* at a small symposium for invited participants from different professional and national backgrounds. The idea was that all "panel" members would watch the full performance at the Jasmin Vardimon Company dance space in Ashford and then be prepared to discuss their immediate reactions to the piece, followed by a more considered short paper response to be delivered the following day. Shortly into the performance one character, Seth Marvell, a group psychotherapist, lies dead after a violent incident in the home of Mimi and Charlie Cain and the subsequent scenes hinge around this death. Throughout the first half, the character of Veronica Hunt, lawyer for the defence, construes the audience as jury. This is done through direct formal addresses to us as such and, prior to the interval, through asking that we retire to consider our verdict.

Six weeks later I undertook two weeks of jury service at a local Crown Court, where, again coincidentally, one of the two cases on which I sat was for domestic violence. The details of the cases are not relevant here and the deliberations of the jury cannot be discussed without being in contempt of court. However, the experience, coming as it did so close to the live viewing of *Justitia*, was provocative, stimulating reflections on both experiences, their puzzling similarities, stark differences and involved questions about truth telling. On the surface both the "juries" were asked to come to a verdict, but it became clear in *Justitia* that this was a dramatic device designed to highlight precisely the impossibility of reaching such an accord. Strands of information about the characters and their hidden anxieties, stories and experiences interwove in increasingly complex and apparently contradictory ways, taking the audience out beyond the immediacy of the tight focus of a trial. Where *Justitia* spilled out, overflowing into multiple potential reasons for the violent action and resulting death, the Crown Court case drew tight boundaries around what was admissible as evidence and influential on jurors' thinking. The arc of the performance was towards unsettling fixed viewpoints and deliberately presenting a range of perspectives, whilst the court case pressed for a single agreed view and decision.

At the core of both events the "jurors" were asked to decide, from contradictory accounts, what was true. In the context of the symposium, this request was readily seen as a fictive device requiring no real agreement on events witnessed or a decision. The result was a stimulating, sometimes argumentative debate that sought to unpick, evaluate and interpret an aesthetic experience. In the Crown Court case, a similar process of interpretive discussion had to lead to agreement (even if that was that no agreement could be reached) and subsequently to instantly life-changing repercussions for participants. However different their anticipated outcomes, the importance of "liveness" in both events was evident, with the contradictory verbal narratives compelling the jurors/audience to find additional means to assess what rang true or hollow. As "ringing true" refers to the testing of the quality of metal or glass through striking it and assessing the sound, it is an apt reminder of the multi-sensory process in which the juror or audience member is engaged. The content of the accounts, that is the words spoken, arrived with undercurrents that could potentially reveal additional or contrasting layers of communication. How are these received and assessed and to what degree do the paralinguistic utterances, tonal quality of voice or movement information, for example, contribute to gauging narratives and their "truths"?

With a background in dance, I was perhaps more focused than most at the *Justitia* symposium on the way dance fused with other arts stimulated a range of senses simultaneously. Similarly, in the Crown Court, the jury members had to draw on the highly textured nature of the courtroom experience to come to a decision. Both situations relied on the juror/audience, creating a scenario or indeed a series of scenarios in their imagination and this imaginative response had to accommodate swift and multiple strands of information assaulting the senses on all sides. Contradictions abounded in the court case. Who was acting their part? How would we deduce that and be sure beyond reasonable doubt? In *Justitia*, all were acting their parts and the impetus of the piece was more towards proliferation of perspectives and how shifts in either viewpoint or narrative thread make the idea of the single truth of an event slip away.

In order to maintain one of the significant guidelines for the *Justitia* panel event – that we respond immediately and then again the next morning – I have included my initial responses in the form of "riffs" as I originally presented them. They therefore "speak" from that event and are, by design, fast and first views or connections to the viewing of the performance. They are separated from the rest of the text with which they re-engage. The term "riffs" was originally employed to indicate significant repetitions of insistent themes. These were the responses to the performance that, next morning, remained most persistent. But in this new context, the term is also applicable to the process that witnesses find themselves in during the court case, with their initial statements made as closely as possible to the crime being considered, re-read in court or virtually re-enacted under cross examination.

RIFF 1 – INNOCENCE

In thinking about this symposium prior to coming, I was bothered that, as I had seen the production before in London (and the DVD several times with undergraduate students who take half a module focusing on the work of the Jasmin Vardimon Company), I would not be able to take a fresh look. A phrase then sprang to mind of movement practitioner Moshe Feldenkrais who, after giving a detailed movement lesson focused on one side of the body, suggesting that when doing the second side the participant comes to the work "innocently". That is that they try to pay attention to the new experience and not limit or pre-judge it by carrying over memories of experience from what they have just done.

To do this in movement is hard but possible. To do this in watching is harder, maybe impossible. But the attempt is liberating.

To attempt to look at something "innocently" makes a greater space to pay attention to the immediate and this is what I did yesterday. The result was a change of focus from the larger narrative drives to the smaller interstitial segments: the moments that escape or refuse the line of direction in order to open out to new terrain. The mystery typist, the solo moments, the trail of Mimi's hand in a water of memories as the stage revolves … The enigma of the typist's knowing dance of looped arms, lusciousness and self-containment, which signalled not innocence, but the weaving of magic spells, charming distractions and divertissements.

Of course the term "innocence" has other resonances for this piece. Was anyone innocent? Or who is manipulating whom?

The concern expressed above, about generating an open focus of awareness in reception prior to watching *Justitia* at the Stour Centre, is remarkably similar to the state required by jurors. Indeed, prior to each case I sat on, the judge invoked the usual stipulation that jurors regard the defendant as innocent unless proven guilty, with the emphasis on the onus of the prosecution to prove guilt, not on the defendant to prove innocence. The explicit advice was therefore to stay open to the information brought into the court and not swiftly pre-judge, either literally through prejudice or through settling on a decision prior to all the evidence being heard.

The name of the performance *Justitia* evokes representations of the Roman goddess, or "Lady Justice" as she has become known, with sword and the scales of justice in hand and, in some instances, with a blindfold over her eyes. The blindfold is a curious image but fits with the idea of coming to an experience "innocently" with an emphasis on the act of listening. In the context of "justice", to listen is to pay attention to people, to witnesses as they relate their experiences, give testimony. Although the emphasis is on sound and therefore verbal recounting, the term "listen" includes the expanded sense of taking heed or attending to someone that could include other sensory information. The blindfold though can also signal a warning, that it is easy to be hoodwinked or led astray. Whichever way it is taken, the powerful visual image acts as a reminder of the need to have full attention, to be alert to both narratives and their method of delivery.

It is this last point that was so compelling in both the performance and the court case. The similarly receptive states, required of spectator and juror, were not for the same purpose. The stripped back nature of the juror's duty was to refuse connective and external information that might generate suppositions or assumptions beyond the facts provided in the courtroom. Within the *Justitia* panel each individual response was to be personal, related to our field and publically expressed in a form (round table, followed by panel) that was both stimulating and pressurised by time constraints. As a juror, my duty was as part of a collective, with all deliberations secret, anonymous and with no set timing. The personal was subsumed into the group's service. So far so different, but what I had not anticipated was the degree to which the evidence in the court case would rely so significantly not on hard facts but on contrasting narratives and nuance of delivery, bringing it much closer to my experience of the performance.

RIFF 2 – MANIPULATION

The early image of the rug suggests double sidedness and duplicity. The plain back, dull and simple, reversed to reveal complex woven patterns, secret codes might be hidden in this. Who can decipher? Who signals to whom? There is a pivotal moment when both sides of the rug are shown as it forms Mimi's wedding dress; a dress made and held forcefully in place by Mr Cain, who also holds Mimi, like a puppet, forcefully in place. A puppet, a doll, exoticised … Multiple sides yes, but who controls these? Is Mimi re-exoticised in the Kung Fu fighting flight, or, as animal defender of her young?

Temporal and spatial manipulation travels through the whole performance. Time frames and bordered spaces are open to incursion and slippage. Throughout there is a glorious irony in the endless focus on doors in the open stage space. A reminder perhaps of the way the mind functions through selective focus. How do we cope with the onslaught of simultaneous experience through every moment of the day? By settling into habitual thought patterns? By going with the driving insistence of narrative?

The juror too is ever aware of the potential to be manipulated as argument swings to and fro. Leaving aside for now the rigid angle each lawyer wishes to present, the memory of witnesses is so imperfect that the juror's imaginary construction of events hovers unsteadily between a series of minutely altered disclosures. To "tell the truth" does not mean to always get every detail correct. In this way the staging of *Justitia* was evocative of the courtroom experience, since the design element of segmented circular stage set on a revolve, as it turned, provoked just that experience of viewing and re-viewing the same scene but with something changed each time. The designs, set so neatly within each stage segment: a living room, a courtroom, a therapeutic space etc., just would not stay in place, but seeped and bled into each other. In the Crown Court, listening to one witness after another describe the same spaces where events took place set up a similarly complex series of images. Sometimes they conformed to each other but very often they did not.

Justitia contains more written text than any other of the Company's pieces, but this is distributed across the performance in a variety of ways: from realistic conversation to formal address or screen projected typing apparently taking place in real time. The author/auteur is presented as the arch manipulator but with so many conflicting views offered and additional storylines, I rapidly lost interest in my constructed role as juror. Emotional back stories, denials, new lines of evidence or fresh segments to the central action began to pall as their number increased. In that sense it was like the crime story in which the denouement was dependent on completely fresh information that could not possibly be puzzled out through clues gleaned along the way. Yet my attention was never lost and, just as in the Crown Court, where the statements of events directly contradicted each other, my focus had spread and shifted to other telling signs.

In a short chapter on global aphasia, clinical neurologist Dr Oliver Sacks notes that his patients with the severest examples of this condition could no longer understand words;

yet, when they listened to the President's speech they laughed and this despite the fact that others without the condition seemed moved by his words. Sacks suggests that their humorous response could not be to the words but to the experience of "*utterance* – an uttering-forth of one's whole meaning with one's whole being – the understanding of which involves infinitely more than mere word-recognition" (1986: 77). Sacks' conclusion is that someone suffering from severe global aphasia can gain an enhanced ability to sense and decode the non-verbal levels of expression involved in natural speech and that they therefore become hard to lie to. They laughed at the speech because they saw through the deceptions by responding to "vocal nuance, the tone, the rhythm, the cadences, the music, the subtlest modulations, inflections, intonations, which can give – or remove – verisimilitude to or from a man's voice" (p. 78). Add to this a similar range of visual cues in facial and bodily expression and the juror, even without such enhanced skills, has a wide array of sensory information with which to assess what rings true. In the performance panel there was no necessity to come to agreement on our interpretations of the piece arising from multi-sensory experience. In the Crown Court, there was every incentive to find consensus, and despite the different social, cultural and age backgrounds we represented, agreement was found readily.

Amidst the mass of information in the court case, clearly some things rang true to a diverse group, or were we all perfectly manipulated, blindfolded like Lady Justice? Without being able to verify events through direct presence there always remains a place of doubt, however tiny, and it is this uncertainty that is prised open in *Justitia*. The group movement sequences reference the content of the spoken or projected text but more importantly bring textures, rhythms and dynamics that expand the performance beyond the words and mimetic narrative. In the "all rise" court sequence, all characters jump on chairs as instruction to rise is given and perform a series of pacey, cyclical movements that take them back to sitting, rolling across the chairs and sidling out of the room only to enter again at the other end of the chair line. Performed in perfect unison whilst maintaining role distinctions, this danced moment broadens the context of the narrative through using repetition and joint action to take the focus beyond individuals to the notion of justice itself. All are caught up in the formality of a repeated and compulsory routine, but the energy and force of the action sweeps out beyond the behavioural norm of the court, catching instead, the intensity of emotional inner experience, which protocol and manners of the system have failed to subsume. Other similarly high octane danced scenes bring passionate experience to the fore, whether, as expected, in the group therapy room or unexpected as in the domestic setting of sitting room, neighbour's house or the lawyer's bedroom.

Instead of pushing the narrative forward these highly charged but sporadic danced sequences provide space for thought and feeling. The imagery they provide is provocative and complex as increasingly obvious meanings are disturbed. At one point the performers begin to climb over the walls of the segmented stage space or are caught frozen for a moment on the legs of the chairs that protrude from the wall. This tilting of perspective and refusal to conform to the usual boundaries afforded by walls brings in an anarchic quality. This, for me, exposes the inner, uncontainable life of the characters and debunks any notion of singular or final "truth" in what we witness. However, in addition, these moments remind us of the power of emotions and how they contribute to viewpoint and ultimately decision making. In *Descartes' Error* neurologist Antonio Damasio argues forcefully for not only recognising the integration of body and mind but also for a re-evaluation of the importance of feelings and emotion within cognitive processing, including decision making. Whilst no decision was required in responding to *Justitia*, this was essential in the Crown Court. According to Damasio's hypotheses, the jury will have come to decisions through a complex process of applying intellectual reasoning helped by feelings. In particular, he postulates that:

> It is likely that as we were being "tuned" in infancy and childhood, most of our decision making was shaped by somatic states related to punishment and reward. But as we matured and repeated situations were categorized, the need to rely on somatic states for every instance of decision making decreased, and yet another layer of automation developed. Decision-making strategies began depending in part on "symbols" of somatic states.
>
> (2006: 184)

Most people (not all, as exemplified by both Sacks and Damasio) have this everyday expertise in evaluating human interaction, but it is an expertise that is so habitual as to largely escape awareness and debate; only exposed for scrutiny in special circumstances such as both the panels discussed here. Using emotional intelligence speeds up decision making and in Damasio's view is far more reliable than attempting to rely on just reasoning and calculation (see Damasio, 2006: 172 for specific illustrations on this).

"Movement never lies" – but of course it does and magnificently so. We do not see military drills in their repetitive dullness and sweaty harshness; we see military drills signalled, up ended, tipped over and performed from every angle, slick and skilled. What lies behind this? Other kinds of physical training looping and cascading into an aesthetic form … "Dance shows emotion" – yes well it can and it does, but also so much more, as in this piece; it tears holes in the text, operates in multiples, is too fast to grasp and hard to memorise unless you dance. It will not conform to the linear. Can any of the many styles of movement offered be trusted over any other? Is the Kung Fu flying fight just the most obvious of the dance illusions that plays with us?

Damasio's research into feelings and emotions and how they are both embodied and integrated into thinking comes with a warning that "symbolic processing may be advantageous or pernicious, depending on the topic and the circumstances" (2006: 184). Both these outcomes were deliberately exploited in *Justitia* to reveal the instability of the single narrative. In the Crown Court case the same could be said to be true but in my estimation the attempt to blind the jury failed.

In the end, in watching *Justitia*, I was drawn back to the dancing. The plot lines and the texts, whether appearing as writing on a screen or spoken between characters, became simultaneously maze-like and, in their linear construction, too simple; they did not ring true. The dance and movement offered something different, textured states that could shift in a second to trigger new connections. The Anonymous Typist, for instance, drew the eye because the action of typing was so quickly insufficient. It was as if she was slipping the bounds of such containment, and as the hands and arms dived and looped through the air a field of reference was created. When the scene returned to her much later, this signature movement grew in sweeping arcs that sculpted the space, signalling her creative role in a more visceral and complex manner than through the words she apparently typed.

I am not so sure that *Justitia* is much about the justice system or a crime at all. In so far as it is, and has the audience play the jury, there are no neat puzzle pieces that will satisfyingly fit together to reveal the murderer. In both this fictive piece and in the case I sat on, the domestic violence took place behind closed doors and with no witnesses, only the main participants could explain what happened. The actual court case was a reminder of the messiness of such trials. Far from the steady build of material evidence, there were just two accounts, two narratives and a decision to be made by twelve ordinary people. But those ordinary people have extraordinary sensory skills that made the decision a clear one, even if you can never be one hundred percent sure it was correct. In reflecting back on *Justitia* after this experience, I appreciate more fully the danced interludes, the movement that confuses, the contradictory and indecisive moments and the stage design that made scenes and individuals' experiences so permeable.

In the Manchester University-based research project "Watching Dance: Kinaesthetic Empathy" the principle investigators pose questions such as: how do "dance spectators respond to and identify with movement [?] To what extent do they internally simulate the movement observed? What conditions favour empathetic response [?]" (Reynolds et al., 2011: npn). These remain fertile questions for debate but in my recent experience perhaps do not go far enough. As jurors in the Crown Court, to what extent did we also experience a degree of kinaesthetic empathy within detailed recollection and retelling of events rather than in the display of movement? To what degree did we rely on the banked experiences of somatic states built up over a lifetime to assess what we witnessed and how restrictive or generative was this in our attempts to "listen" and discover what "rang true"?

RIFF 4 – SPEAKING

Back to behaviour and how it switches and transmutes and is controlled according to the space marked public or private. Who speaks, who is allowed to speak and who speaks for others?

The final questions in this last "riff" are generated by a performance in which characters are exposed in layer after layer of manipulations of each other and of their "jury" audience. But now, in retrospect, perhaps equally pertinent questions arise that concern not just what is spoken but how it is spoken and consequently how the witnesses who, saturated in this multi-sensory experience, listen, watch, feel, are moved, and attempt to deduce what rings true. In the admittedly very different contexts of Crown Court and theatre, it nevertheless felt like a privilege to be given time to attend to, and space to voice an opinion on, these life stories. Yet both experiences revealed repeatedly the internally created and externally enforced mechanisms that threaten to deny freedom of expression. Considered in conjunction with one another, this theatrical performance and court case expose societal structures of power that overtly and covertly control who can speak and when. Yet both experiences buzzed with the tension of resisting such constraints, as movement, tones and textures combined with words to press the "juries" into listening. To experience an account as "ringing true" is to rely on embodied and emotionally intelligent assessment of the kind suggested by Sacks and Damasio. But, to believe utterly in this "truth" is to override the multiple perspectives that *Justitia* offers as passionate reminders that truths are never quite stable but always contingent on a new view, context or indeed, a feeling.

Seen by Me, It Writes

Felix Ensslin

FIRST RESPONSE

As I type these words "first response" I realise they are meant as a kind of tracking number signifying nothing but rather keeping one's senses trained on a trace. Nevertheless, without being descriptive or communicating any sense of the piece I just saw, they take me straight to …, well, if not into the middle of things then at least into the muddle of things. "First Responders" is a term out of the emergency service play book. It refers to those equipped to be first on a scene of an accident or crime. Their purpose is to save lives or secure the scene of a crime. Naturally, theatre has always been tied to that scene. It conjures the dead as the dead conjure guilt. It used to, at least. And it stages crimes so enormous, any discourse of fact and value, any reading of the traces with the detective's nose close to the ground, may never quite reach it. The enormity of the crime is never its scale. It is its link to desire. This is the reason: crime is always linked to the scandal of the body, which never just figures, but writes. Thus dance, thought once - along with the chorus - to be a taming of the abysmal renunciation of all separation and individuality, in some way is always also dancing on a grave.

FIRST: "RESPONSE"

Justitia: Goddess of justice and allegory. With the need for gendered translation (which to us heirs of monotheism always already has the quality of the bygone as well as conjuring up the heathen and thus sexualised imagination) a focus is directed to the "a" designating femininity. Turning to the *personae*: while the lawyer woman upholds phallic justice and the ideal of perfect and conscious recreation of the past by reading all the traces properly as signs, the sign being read by the performance itself is this "a". Not justice, but *Justitia*.

The scales that matter here are those of musical scores, driving rhythms, movement. Nothing is put in the scales to balance the fate that desire is writing. It *writes*, because it *responds*: Mimi to the soldier's gesture of helping the children she teaches, the soldier to his calling, the therapist to the fashions of his trade. Desire, so it has been said, always is the desire of the other. A genitive you can read subjectively and objectively; desiring the other, desiring what the other desires. Desiring the other's desire for oneself. Dance thus emerges as movement hanging on a threat dangling from the waste of signification, the letter.

JUSTITIA

Justice enters through a scene. The *Orestie* shows us how, through Athena's intervention, the bloody law of revenge is substituted by the law … period. In the Old Testament it is the monotheistic god that makes revenge his privilege, thus ending the endless and frenzied feuds of blood revenge. Something is lost by this introduction of a third position: the law, God, Athena, *Justitia*. Lost is immediacy and retaliation, that is "first response". If wronged, hold your breath and wait. Or rather, don't hold your breath, but count the traces, as signs to be presented to the Other, so that the order of *Justitia* may affirm itself, thus reaffirming order … period. Thus, *Justitia*, having been waited upon and waited on, creates an audience: for the count needs to be heard for it to count. If there is no immediate reaction to a wrong, the wrong becomes a crime and the place of its appearance becomes a crime scene. Now the community becomes an audience and thus its members become citizens. Their lot is to be breathlessly waiting for the next chapter to unfold. The climax will be the court drama, from the mousetrap to *Boston Legal*. Once we substitute revenge for the law, there is an audience.

WITNESSES

And there are witnesses – testimony of witnesses that seems to help in establishing fact, but actually starts by interpreting what counts as fact. This "counting as" is at stake whenever there is an audience. When I see, hear, taste something "as something" it starts to exist. This is a form of validation, yes, but it's not just the old "fact" and "value" dichotomy (or "denotation" and "connotation", "objective" and "subjective" - there are many ways this has been written). And wherever it has been written it was tied up with something else, whether knowingly or unknowingly. Behind "fact" and "value" lies the dichotomy of "reason" and

124

"feeling", "man" and "woman", "white" and "not white" in all their forms. The birthmark of art has always been this: if it makes itself the witness of something beyond reason, of something before language, of something outside thought, then art acquiesces into this heritage. Namely, to be the other of reason, of whiteness, of maleness, of logos, whatever. So when the witness starts to hear, see, taste, feel something "as something", more is at stake than this validation of a dichotomy between reason and feeling, the objective and subjective. Or rather, more should be at stake.

RESPONSIBILITY

The dimension of being a witness that is opened up when we create this scene of *Justitia* realises this: she is making … well, us. *Justitia* is making us a scene. The scene is that *Justitia* is making us. How? If it is not only a supplement to reason, not only reasons other than we encounter when we encounter "physical" responses tied to the body and sensations, but rather something repetitive, an insistence reaching from the past and the future, it must be something like this: a something that counts as the basis or cause of both reason and what counts for sensations, feelings, something at least logically prior. What could this be? It's maybe something like repetition itself and the fact that while we cannot control it, we are responsible for it. The woman typing at the beginning of the scenes of Jasmin Vardimon's play shows this to be the case. It starts with the fact is that we are not only responsible to report the facts that we see, but for what we see as facts. There is no "meta-position" from which to first count everything that belongs to the order of fact and then select what elements of that order are present at the moment of witnessing. Rather, it is prior to the meeting of subject and object that we are responsible for choosing the position of the subject, the subjective position, which makes us count what counts.

FIRST RESPONDERS

Not saving lives, not securing a scene: or, rather, doing both? Witnessing we are always first responders, choosing before seeing what to see, before hearing what to hear, before feeling what to feel. Narration is always secondary: a kind of waste product, trying to make a unity where there certainly can never be one. But also trying to establish perspectives, where there aren't any, because the choice of subjective position has always already been made. The hard part is this: this choice does not allow us to take up a meta-position from which to survey the rest and confidently state one's place in the whole. The hole in the narrative is constitutive of the scene, any scene. That is true definitely also of the scene that *Justitia* is making us. She dances around it, thankfully.

Hiding in Plain View

Christine Harmar-Brown

Nothing is straightforward, nothing is as it seems and everything is a matter of interpretation.

The Writer sits at her typewriter and writhes as the story flows from her to the machine, or is it the other way around? What follows is, in part, an illustration of the act of story making. An association of images, characters and situations creates a narrative. Like chicken and egg it is hard to distinguish which comes first: the image or the idea, the cause or the consequence? We, the audience, respond intellectually and emotionally. The collective weight of our cultural and emotional references has, for so long, been shone back at us through the vast array of interpretive media (film, newspapers, music, television, art) that it is worth considering to what extent our emotions are as received as our opinions.

As a writer, *Justitia* intrigues me on several levels. The combination of genres employed to tell an essentially simple story has a Brechtian effect. We, the audience, are periodically reminded that we are witnessing a story, a construct. Not only this, we are also obliged to adjust our expectations according to the genre being employed. As audiences we are experts and have general expectations of the genres we are familiar with. A love story will tug at our heart-strings, a folktale may warn us, a courtroom drama will intrigue us and so forth.

The title of the piece *Justitia*, and the contexts of the courtroom and trial, places the idea of justice at the forefront of our minds. As an audience we are invited to act as a kind of "super jury", forming opinions not only about the guilt or innocence of the accused, but also of the veracity of the process. By using different genres to present the prosecution and defence "stories", the audience is prompted to consider to what extent a jury's ability to interpret events and administer justice is compromised by culturally defined preconceptions.

An encrypted woven rug forms a magic carpet to transport two young lovers. This is a familiar feature of folk stories. Despite their contemporary characteristics (he is a British soldier, she is a medical student from Hong Kong) we understand that they are innocents abroad, neither of them in their own environment and, as such, they have a slightly mythic quality. We do not know too much about them. To an extent they are everyman and our expectation is that the story will contain challenges that will either overcome or defeat the couple and, in so doing, teach us something about the nature of love.

At first they are gentle with each other, their love blossoms and they decide to marry but this fairy-tale mood is soon shattered, the tone changes, becomes gritty and urban. We witness scenes from the soldier's past, his role in active service, possible flashbacks from a war zone.

Back in England, the soldier and his buddy reminisce: blood, bullets and football. The young wife seems almost forgotten, a shadowy figure in her new home. Her husband drinks beer with his best mate; they shout, drunkenly at the TV screen as they watch a match, caricatures, macho stereotypes. The warning signs are there, we are trained to spot them, know there is trouble brewing, and when the soldier's young wife is accused of the murder of his buddy we might be satisfied: we understand where we are. We might project the story into any number of combinations found in any melodrama or soap opera, all of which are supported by our prejudices and preconceptions. We understand the clichés because we make them: soldiers who cannot leave the violence behind, post-traumatic stress disorder, difficulties with assimilation for the young wife.

A courtroom is assembled. Jurors seem to be tested by a gruelling, parodic burst of musical chairs, leaping, straight backed, off and onto hard wooden chairs. The legs of the chairs having previously been slotted through slits in the walls, slits that evoke the inspection windows of cell doors and through which harsh beams of blue white light are shone.

Several versions of events are revealed. The husband goes out to the shop leaving his wife and friend behind at home. In one version, the young wife seduces her husband's friend, is rejected by him and lashes out in fury. In another, the friend forces himself upon her and she lashes out in self-defence. How do we discover the truth, determine guilt, see justice done? Is one version of events more compelling than another? Why? Do we find one account, one set of facts more plausible? Is this because they resonate more with our own experiences, expectations or preconceptions? If the jury is made up of people like us, the audience, then how can they remain impartial?

Not only are we being asked to question the notion of justice, our emotional engagement, our sense of how real this is, is being challenged. Are we to believe this really happened? One version of events is brutally graphic; it looks real; it feels real. When the friend rapes the young wife, the audience is caught in the moment like a fish on a hook. However, the next moment we witness the exquisitely executed slow motion graphic of a cartoon revealing the same sequence of events. But this time there is no shock; we don't worry this might be real, instead we enjoy the spectacle. So now we ask ourselves if the manner in which we receive ideas or information is more potent than the idea itself. We are given recognisable cultural signposts, one after another, and end up knowing we are lost within their conflicting messages.

So far so good. We understand we are being asked to consider the relativity of truth and justice, the work is called *Justitia* after all. But notice the other drama playing out around the jury, the witnesses, the neighbour. This drama concerns the dialogue you are having with yourself about one of the characters. The neighbour is a woman, she has long hair and she wears a skirt but …. You think she's a man. You know the character is a woman but the dancer is a man, but why? Is it polite to ask the question? Is this down to the gender politics of women in crime? How do you read this? Why are you trying to convince yourself he is a women? "Look at that sportswomen, Caster Semenya", you think, "she looks like a man". Then look at his/her face. S/he knows you know s/he knows you know and s/he is challenging you, s/he is playing with you. How far will you go to collude with an idea?

Now the audience has been manoeuvred into a more urgent relationship with the work. This is not about recognising genres or understanding Brechtian alienation: this is about you and your prejudices. There are no clues, there is no context to explain the imagery, there is no reason for the character of this woman to be played by a man and it is as real as seeing a man in drag on the street. How you respond to this will show you how many hurdles justice must negotiate.

Putting Clouds in Boxes
Paul Brill

I am a criminal defence lawyer, and look at *Justitia* from that perspective. The courtroom as theatre, the wiles of lawyers within the legal system and their cynical disregard for the "truth" are all well-visited areas in novels, plays and film. *Justitia* makes its own visit but examines the complexities within a system that necessarily has to deal with shifting realities of human behaviour and motivation. There are two aspects of *Justitia* I would like to reflect on here: the first is focused on the movement at the beginning of the piece by an anonymous typist, and the second is the portrayal of the defence advocate.

There was an asymmetry to the movement of the anonymous typist, a combination of a very firm "ratatatat" of the typing - metronomic, certain and unyielding - and a rather fluid and flowing movement that emerged from the left side, led by the left hand. This movement was as if the typist was hearing music, so that at times there was a suggestion of conducting. This combination works on one level as a metaphor for working within the criminal trial process itself insofar as it reflects a combination of an appreciation of the fluid, shifting complexities of human behaviour with a hard-edged pragmatic need to find a way towards resolution of cases.

In the criminal trial process a number of difficult, shifting and amorphous concepts are dealt with. The first and most obviously difficult of concepts is that of trying to work out what is going on in someone's head, looking into the defendant's mind and having to distinguish between concepts such as what a person intends as opposed to what they want or merely desire. This is attempted from consideration of what is said and how people are shown to have acted. Decisions may have to be made about, for example, how someone has acted in reaction to provocation and what was the final trigger for the action. Such concepts are difficult enough. Applying them in a practical context is particularly difficult.

What is in a person's mind has relevance within the context of a framework of established facts. This may be thought to provide some certainty in building parameters within which there will be further considerations. It might be thought that establishing those parameters is relatively straightforward but that is not necessarily the case. There can be disputes – not just about what actually did happen, but disputes over, for example, the significance of scientific evidence. Experts can disagree, so establishing where the parameters are in a criminal trial may not be straightforward. Having said that there will often be a set of accepted facts: "pillars" around which competing narratives snake. When it comes to the assessment of those narratives (usually two but sometimes more), much, maybe all, will depend on the view taken of the credibility and/or reliability of different witnesses. There are rules that are imposed. For example, juries may or may not be told about someone's previous convictions, and if they are told there are rules about how they treat those previous convictions.

Notwithstanding all of that, much will depend on an assessment about how particular witnesses are regarded, and how well what they say fits in with what is known. There has to be an understanding of these complexities that lie behind any trial, and something that *Justitia* does is to appreciate this in a clear way by showing alternative narratives that, to greater or lesser extents, fit perfectly with the facts as they are known.

This complexity can also be seen in the therapy scene in which there is the monologue by a woman who spoke about her responsibility for the death of a child. It was not clear whether she was absolutely criminally liable. At different times she expressed remorse, defiance ("… it's not my responsibility") and a raw sense of being haunted by the fact of the child's death, or by the child herself. The other members of the therapy group respond in ways (sometimes comic) to her lurches between different responses to her part in a tragedy. To be clear about where responsibility lay is challenging. The scene had the texture and mess of truth about it.

But if the truth can be messy how are trials to be resolved? That texture and mess and the amorphous nature of what can come before the courts has to be coped with. Hard lines have to be drawn. Concepts of motivation and uncertainty within a relevant factual context must be contained. A resolution that fully reflects the nuances and shifting complexities of a given situation can only rarely be achieved. The cloud has somehow to be put into a box. Hard lines must be drawn for reasons of pragmatism. Within an adversarial system the trial process is not an enquiry into the truth, it is an enquiry into whether someone can be proved to be guilty or not. A defendant is found to be guilty or *not guilty*. It is not a question of being found guilty or *innocent*, and so these things have to be dealt with in a very pragmatic way. *Justitia* is interesting in the way that it understands that and the initial conflicted movement of the anonymous typist that triggered these reflections seemed to contain that understanding.

The second aspect that I want to explore was the representation of the defence advocate herself as again there is an interesting conflict. On the one hand, there is the classic popular culture picture of the criminal advocate as the manipulator of the jury. This is exemplified in the musical *Chicago* with that advocate celebrating how he gives the jury the "razzle dazzle". The portrayal of the advocate in *Justitia* reflected that very well and very entertainingly, for example in the section where she was painting the neighbour witness with lurid make-up and "puppeting" her to say what she wanted her to say, and to be who she needed her to be in front of the jury. There was one scene where she was showing the jury a possible scenario and putting the shirt back on the illicit male lover and generally doing what, in popular culture, advocates in those circumstances do. She is willing to use her wiles. When she was speaking to the audience as jurors, she didn't say "I'm going to wrap you around my finger"; she was going to "wrap you around my *shapely* finger". She was celebrating her gift for the "razzle dazzle".

Against all of that the movement suggested vulnerability, and particularly getting sucked in. Ultimately the point was reached where we saw her preparing the case in bed, suggesting an involvement leading to vulnerability at a personal level; for the advocate had otherwise been shown to be an arch manipulator who revelled in her capacity for, and ability in, such dark arts.

The notion of the cynical, calculating lawyer with a sad/difficult/flawed/torrid private life is a well-trodden path in popular fiction, but in *Justitia* there is the suggestion of a deeper, more corrosive influence of the role of the lawyer on the person of the lawyer … let me think about that.

A Choreography of Words: Reflections on *Justitia*

Amanda Stuart Fisher

25TH SEPTEMBER 2014

When preparing this text for publication I faced a dilemma. As I clicked open the document I'd written on 23rd February 2012, I realised with some horror that I couldn't remember very much about what I'd said about Jasmin Vardimon's *Justitia*. Having been invited to a symposium to see and discuss the work, at the end of the first day we were sent home with instructions to write about what we'd seen. The train ticket receipt reminded me of the date I'd seen the production and I could certainly remember the journey to and from Kent and the strange but exciting delirium of trying to write a response to a piece of performance overnight. But try as I might, I could not remember the text that I actually wrote. The production itself still retained an impression in my memory, but I realised that the detail had faded and what remained was a series of moments, bite-sized aesthetic memories that were activated when I read what I'd written and which then became punctums to the more quotidian memories I have about the day: finding the venue, sitting in the brightly lit space watching the performance begin, the lunch we had and my journey home where I began typing immediately in great fear that I wouldn't get the text finished on time.

Peggy Phelan argues that performance is constituted by the inevitability of its *disappearance* and argues that "in a strict ontological sense [performance] is nonreproducive" (2001: 148). Other performance theorists, however, have argued against this stance and have suggested that after the performance something remains and/or performance itself is not as singular and un-reproductive as Phelan would have us believe. Diana Taylor, for example, suggests that performance has the capacity to capture, or echo, that which once *was there* but which is no longer *present*. She argues that "performance makes visible (for an instant, live now) that which is always already there: the ghosts, the tropes, the scenarios that structure our individual and collective life" (2003: 143). In this way, performance – for Taylor – attests

135

to a life that was once lived, and to the values and beliefs that became inscribed in that time. Rebecca Schneider considers "disappearance" of performance from a different perspective and argues against the binary distinction that positions the text as dead and easily reproductive and performance as live and unrepeatable. Instead, she suggests that texts too can become subject to a revision and "choreographic" shifting that occurs when they are read by others and are cited or mis-cited. She says:

> Dwelling in the dust, texts themselves necessarily meet bodies and engage in the repetition and revision, the citing and becoming that is also choreography, orature, song.
>
> (2011: 106)

I would argue that we could also think about the process of writing about performance as a performative act of *remembering*. It is an action that takes place in the present, but it is one that is engaged with a retrieval of the past. Like any memory process the remembering of performance engages the author in an intersubjective tangle both with the selfhood of the author and with the event itself, and as I try to recall the performance of *Justitia*, my subjective sense of my own self and my own memories merges with the piece itself. Writing about *Justitia* then becomes a process of trying to try to knit together and unravel what I know I saw and my memory of it.

As I type together a text that will essentially stand in for this act of memory and bear witness to what is recalled, I become acutely aware of what – in a click of the keyboard – becomes omitted and what is included. I struggle to remember the names of the characters, for example, and I no longer can recall whether we find out who did what at the end.

And yet, as I read back over what I wrote over two years ago, I realise that what emerges today is actually a choreography of words that in many ways illuminate Schneider's, Taylor's and Phelan's texts.

Firstly, the performance has definitively vanished. Even when I watch the DVD of the production in an effort to remind myself of what I have now lost, I feel a sense of estrangement and 'goneness'. The video-ed *Justitia* is a different performance; I can no longer hear the breath of the dancers or the thud of their footsteps. I no longer gasp at their physical prowess or wonder how they manage to pull off such virtuoso moves. The screen cuts me off from the spine-tingling moments of physical agility and extraordinary skill. Furthermore, the cast has changed and in fact as the video dance piece continues I feel myself begin to view the piece as if I'm watching something completely different.

Secondly, the original text that I wrote following the performance (and which is presented below) now contains its own "choreography" of marks, traces, memories and inscriptions for me; they appear in the form of a palimpsest – as sedimented into layerings of meaning and opacity. As I read it, I am transported to another time that is one of uncertainty, of neither knowing nor not knowing. Within the text I detect the ghostly remains of myself and that strange glimmer of thought processes, which is both familiar and unfamiliar. It bears the evidence of the texts I was reading and the research I was engaged in just before I came to the *Justitia* symposium. Here one confronts the problem of writing about performance, which is also the performance of writing – with its own "ontology" of the text that bears within it the disappearance of the moment of its inscription. It is where different and seemingly unrelated texts from different times collide and interweave with my memory of a remarkable dance performance: *Justitia*. And so what follows is a text written on the night of 23rd February 2012. It is not the dance piece itself, of course – and yet the performance of *Justitia* is interwoven into it and echoes throughout; even if it is ghostly and barely visible. The text speaks of the past, but it also speaks of my own 'pastness' before the performance of *Justitia* began. In this way, the problematic explored in *Justitia* reflects the act of writing about performance itself. Like the witness in *Justitia*'s courtroom scenes whose veracity we question, writing about performance reminds us that memory is fallible and like testimony it is always subjective. Yet, like the act of witnessing, remembering a performance should also be understood as having a truth claim attached to it, because like the witness, the author promises to speak truthfully, but a text – like testimony – is always bound by the witness's own unique subject position. Similarly, the author can only present an impression of a performance and any account will also reveal the trace memories and the selfhood of the author herself. Furthermore, I'm conscious that the text that is printed below will also come to shift and change in the mind of the reader, as the other contributions shift and change your perspective of what *Justitia* was about and how it was remembered.

23RD FEBRUARY 2012

We are presented with a woman typing. The clitter clatter of the typewriter keys are echoed in a series of movements. One of her hands types while the other arm moves in a syncopated movement following the rhythm of the keys and marking out a translucent dance of words where meaning immediately dissolves and rhythms become both simultaneously meaningful and meaningless. As this moment develops, I find myself asking who is controlling whom here. Is this performer writing the story that is going to be told to us in this performance, or is this story in fact writing her? And what is it that connects Jasmin Vardimon, the auteur and choreographer of this piece, with the narratives that emerge to be explored and then subsequently dismantled by the company who perform them? The words that, on the one hand, seem to become *present* and *material* through the sonic reverberations of the typewriter soon dissipate, and the writing of the typewriter merges with the embodied movement of the dancer, interwoven but also indissoluble.

The ideas that emerge in these early moments stay with me as the piece takes the audience through a continuously playful encounter of the discordance between the material content of the narrative and the materiality of the performance itself. The piece presents us with what – at least on the surface – appears to be a quest for the truth: was this murder, manslaughter, self-defence? However, as an audience, we become positioned simultaneously as both the jurors of the case and as an outsider of the jury or rather as outside of the juridical process itself. The question that emerges is "Are we merely spectators?" Or, do we also become involved in a process of authorship – piecing together the fragments of competing narratives in order to find a "truth" that we can commit to and believe in? The framing of the courtroom certainly appeals to our desire to find out "what happened" and somewhat tantalisingly it appears to offer the promise (an ultimately illusory one, as it turns out) of a coherent and factual truth.

And in a way, I would argue, in this piece it is the possibility of fact as truth that is tried and tested on the stand. We are presented, for example, with the "fact" of DNA evidence being found upon the rug. Yet, this "factual" evidence ultimately fails to answer the bigger question of why one person would kill another. Certainly, within a court of law truth is generally conceived as fact and it is factual truth that informs the integrity of any western juridical system that is built on a collectively held, constitutive trust in due process. As Robert Summers, a research professor in law, explains:

A primary function of trial court procedures (which I will also call adjudicative processes) and of rules of evidence in cases before courts in which facts are in dispute is to find the truth …. without judicial findings of fact that generally accord with truth, citizens would, over time, lose confidence in adjudicative processes as fair and reliable tribunals of justice and as effective means of dispute resolution.

(1999: 497)

Similarly, from a philosophical perspective, fact is traditionally conceived as that which corresponds to how the world actually is: facts describe what *is the case*. A factual statement then becomes true only in that it accurately corresponds to what actually *is* in the world: "It is raining" becomes factually true when we go outside and get wet. In this sense of the assertion, the words that are stated as a "truth" correspond in an untroubled way to what is empirically given as fact.

Yet as *Justitia* moves on from this early moment where the young woman is almost choreographically inscribed by her own story and her own self-narration of it (i.e. in the typing), the question of what kind of truth this performance will disclose is thrown wide open.

Furthermore, we also begin to question the role that words and narrative plays in a recounting and remembering of an event, not only within the juridical process itself, but also in the way that we come to know ourselves and how we experience our being in the world. This is encapsulated for me most clearly in the performance of the clitter clatter of the typing that reads:

> *I type therefore I am*
> *I am therefore I type.*

Here I found myself beginning to reflect on what might be described as a dialectic relationship between the material of the play and the materiality of its performance. What I mean by this is that in Vardimon's unique approach to what we might call physical dance theatre we simultaneously encounter the *affect* of a highly aesthetic choreography as well as momentary instances of *characterisation* where the bodies that move before us instantly and momentarily perhaps become a "character". Certainly as the piece develops we become aware that certain performers are representing certain characters at particular times. But, in an echo of the dissonances between and within the concepts of fact, truth and law, the representational labour of this mimetic substitution is also consistently and playfully troubled – the lawyer becomes the puppet master of the witness, Mimi Kim shifts from one type of person to another (demure wife, rape victim, Kung Fu expert). In other words, throughout the piece the very possibility of words providing a way towards a transparent access to the truth of the event is itself troubled. In psychoanalysis, words – through a narrative process of remembering – become the means by which a past event is processed and *worked through*. Freud considers it a "therapeutic triumph" (2006: 397) when the therapist "successfully uses the remembering process to resolve an issue that the patient would rather get rid of in the form of an action" (p. 397). However, in *Justitia*, the connection between the past event and what becomes iterated is itself problematised and we observe a group therapy session where the analysands refuse to tell their story, choosing instead to present different accounts of "what happened". These are re-presented to us before being summarily dismissed as fabrications and lies, leaving us to reflect on the fragility of the material "facts" of the case, and our desire to believe the testimony of the victim, as she emerges in the rape scene, for example.

Through the interplay of dancers who occasionally speak to us but who also engage in an athletic, aesthetic movement, any unified and reliable sense of character dissolves and one story seems to bleed into another, as one moment infects another. Through this dissonance we begin to see how a version of the past emerges and is presented in order to speak to a future while always engaging in the constantly shifting ground of the present. However, significantly perhaps, because of the narrative tropes that frame the piece as a whole, the characters of Mimi Kim, Charles Cain and Mr Marvell do not dissipate completely; they remain neither present nor not present. Instead we might say these characters emerge almost as ghostings. They become present through the performance of their absence and the slippage between the many different competing narratives and truths.

We are not, however, allowed to simply fall into relativism here. The possibility of a truth conceived only in terms of individual perception and subjective perspective is refused by a constant playfulness about the status of guilt in the case. The question of guilt becomes a means of drawing attention to a paradoxical tension underpinning the piece: the desire to know what happened and the way "truth" in a juridical context immediately implies culpability. In this way the piece stages the impossibly of remaining in a state that Derrida might describe as a position of *undecidability*. We do not know but we also cannot not need to know. Equally, a sense of guilt emerges not as something that we choose as a rational response to a situation, but as that which pricks our conscience reminding or even alerting us to the possibility that we are denying or betraying a particular truth. In his essay *Demeure: Fiction and Testimony* (2000), which examines the possibility of making a distinction between testimony and truth, fiction and autobiography, Derrida reminds us that however difficult it is to determine where truth ends and fiction begins, we cannot remain indifferent about it. He says:

> One thus finds oneself in a fatal and double impossibility: the impossibility of deciding, but the impossibility of *remaining* [demeurer] in the undecidable.
>
> (p. 16)

The moment of this impossibility of deciding is – in my view – most brutally performed in the account of the killing of the three-year-old girl and, specifically, in the moment when the body hits the car, which I think she describes as something like – "not a loud thud but one that was very real". As we observe the driver deciding whether to stay and confront this act or leave the scene in order to remember it only as "a dream", we confront the ethical imperative of decisiveness and therefore we must face the possibility that the truth and culpability still matters.

The last moment I would like to reflect on is the final confession of Mimi Kim. What are we to make of this moment? Is this an explanation? Is this a moment of revelatory significance? I found myself drawn here to research in legal spheres on the power of confession. In an article written by Saul M. Kassin and Katherine Neumann in the journal *Law and Human Behaviour* (1997), they argue that when a confession is introduced into a court case, whether or not it is claimed to be acquired under coercion, it still holds a powerful sway vis-à-vis the believability of a witness. Leading Kassin and Neumann to state that "… many legal scholars have, on the basis of intuition, ranked confession as highest of the scale of evidence" (1997: 471).

Confessions, it seems, produce the highest conviction rates and are understood to be the most incriminating evidence, followed by the eye witness and character testimony. Dramaturgically, the confession of Mimi Kim suggests a moment of revelation and therefore a "truth". Yet, as jurors we do not witness this account directly as its actual content is communicated only through translation. For most of us in the audience, the sense of Mimi Kim's words remains indiscernible and the confession becomes a performance only, marked by its opacity it becomes a moment of *affect*. There is a sense that this is a confession. Yet, there is also the possibility that we – as jurors – are simply being manipulated by a dramaturgical structure and the performance of this moment, raising further questions about the status of truth in the context of testimony and the performativity of the witness in the act of confession.

Authorship, Physical Theatre and *Justitia*

Royona Mitra

INTRODUCTION

In this chapter I examine the importance of authorship in *Justitia* (2007) and contextualise my analysis in relation to conceptual debates surrounding authorship within the genre of physical theatre. My key aim is to unpick the creative and philosophical tensions that characterise performance-making processes in physical theatre, as they oscillate between conventional hierarchies of directing and more collaborative devising methodologies. I argue that in *Justitia* these innate tensions of authorship are borne out in two ways. Firstly, in its metaphoric manifestations in a courtroom drama that constantly make the audience question whose stories they are witnessing, who authors and relays them and their authenticities. Secondly, and perhaps more significantly, through suggesting a dialectical relationship between the authorship of the piece's narrative, and the complex nature of authorship in the genre of physical theatre itself. These two perspectives are fundamentally intertwined, much like my own responses to two separate performances of *Justitia* on which this study rests. The first as witnessed at Lichfield Garrick Theatre in April 2009 and the second as witnessed at Stour Centre in Ashford, the home of Jasmin Vardimon Company (JVC), in February 2012. In the former performance, the character of the anonymous typist, whose crucial role I shall elaborate on later, was created and performed by Jasmin Vardimon, the artistic director of JVC. In a study that examines notions of authorship within the genre of physical theatre through reflections on authorship in and of *Justitia*, this intriguing placement of the author/maker of *Justitia* within the piece itself is worthy of analysis. I argue that, on the one hand, it becomes the fulcrum on which the illusive nature of legal enquiries and its relationship to authorship rests, while, on the other, it becomes an important commentary on the illusive role of an artistic director within a devised and collaborative ensemble.

Illusion, then, appears as a double-edged sword within *Justitia*. It is the fundamental quality that connects the unfolding of the narrative of *Justitia* to the piece's creative process. In other words, we constantly question whose narratives we are witnessing as much as we question who created these narratives in the first place. In such a slippery framework, what can the adoption of the literary term "authorship" bring to our understanding of creative processes within the physical theatre genre? I use the term "authorship" to imply more than the kind of ownership and copyright that can be claimed over a text-based archive such as a novel or a play, which we often attribute to a single author or creator. I signal instead a more complex and heterogeneous network of creative contributions that are generated in responses to creative tasks within workshops, and manifest in gestures or movement sequences or soundscapes and are shared by an ensemble. By authorship I refer here to the generation of an ensemble's shared repertoire that exists largely in corporeal dimensions, and is inherited and embodied through shared physical languages.

In this chapter I shall demonstrate the ways in which *Justitia* embodies a collapse between these two oppositional approaches to "authorship", by revealing the tensions that come into existence when single archival authorship and collaborative repertoire enter into dialogue with each other. These philosophical musings transpire through the metaphor of a conventional courtroom drama that tells the story of a woman (Mimi Cain) who is convicted and tried for the murder of her husband's best friend (Seth Marvell), as the audience is made to assume the role of the jury. *Justitia* presents multiple versions of realities as presented by different perspectives at the trial, such that truth and fiction are blurred. While in the spirit of a legal enquiry we witness the defendant Mimi Cain's story, we are constantly left wondering who is responsible for authoring it. Is it Mimi herself? Is it her defence lawyer Veronica Hunt in her conviction to prove Mimi innocent? Or, is it Cassandra the stenographer, who admits to letting her mind wander as she transcribes truths onto paper, suggesting the easy slippage between fact and fiction. In *Justitia*, through a carefully crafted layering of text, physicality and digital projection, Vardimon creates believable and tangible characters who move with as much clarity, conviction and psychological insight as they speak. Using a script that is developed alongside the devising process by writer Rebecca Lenkiewicz enables Vardimon to layer her characters with details where the language of gestures falls short. More significantly, the use of the script raises important questions about the complex nature of authorship in collaborative and devised performance practices such as physical theatre.

I would suggest that in a genre that has been historically generated by an anti-text agenda, the use of the script can in some ways hierarchise and control the means through which meaning is authored and communicated to an audience.

PHYSICAL THEATRE, DEVISING METHODOLOGIES AND AUTHORSHIP

While historically physical theatre as a genre has successfully moved beyond text-centric communication, the amalgamation of movement and text is not an uncommon feature in the genre's more contemporary manifestations, demonstrated in the works of DV8 Physical Theatre, Akram Khan Company, Vincent Dance Theatre and of course JVC. Elusive in itself, the term "physical theatre", and the genre that it stands for, has become highly contested in contemporary performance practice. In recent years several scholars have tried to delineate definitions for the genre by purporting views that rarely overlap (Callery, 2001; Murray and Keefe, 2007; Sánchez-Colberg, 2007), leading to simultaneously operative multiple understandings of the genre. However, they do all concur that over the years the term has lost its "charge" (Murray and Keefe, 2007: 2) as it has increasingly been "used to identify an eclectic production commonly understood to be one which focuses on the unfolding of a narrative through physicalised events and which relegates verbal narrative – if at all present – to a subordinate position" (Sánchez-Colberg, 2007: 21). As identified by Sánchez-Colberg, the broad remit of this description is clearly problematic and has turned the label into a "catch-all phrase" (Callery, 2001: 6) that has come to mean nothing and many things at the same time, making Murray and Keefe wistfully suggest that "perhaps the moment of physical theatre has passed […]" (Murray and Keefe, 2007: 2). Despite these claims, the label and practices claiming it persist, both in academia and in the contemporary performance world. This necessitates a brief summary of its contested genealogy in order to contextualise the practice of JVC and conduct my analysis of *Justitia*.

Franc Chamberlain identifies two primary lineages for the genre in the British context. The first is that of the mime tradition as embodied in the training of Copeau, Decroux and Lecoq, and the second is the aesthetic embodied in the practice of the British company DV8 Physical Theatre and their challenge to contemporary dance (Chamberlain, 2007: 119). He goes on to cite a third lineage to physical theatre in the avant-garde theatre practices of Meyerhold, Artaud and Grotowski, which he proposes was obscured and overshadowed by the practices identified by the label in the 1980s (Chamberlain, 2007: 119). Simon Murray and John Keefe trace the label's multi-lineaged history from the practice of Grotowski in the late 1960s, to Steven Berkoff and his Lecoq-inspired aesthetic in the 1970s, but recognise that it was DV8 Physical Theatre's endorsement of the label in its company name in 1986 that made it a popular label (Murray and Keefe, 2007: 14). In order not to demonstrate a preference towards a specific lineage, Murray and Keefe employ a pluralistic approach to the genre by claiming for physical theatres or the physical in theatres (2007: 1). They identify a commonality amongst these varied lineages as practices "rooted in certain through-lines of principles of theatre itself; of embodied ideas that are in a *dialectical* relationship to the spoken word" (2007: 3). There is of course an inherent problem in embracing such a pluralistic position as it foregoes the opportunity to identify the philosophical and aesthetic intersections that characterise the genre. This is rectified by dance scholar Ana Sánchez-Colberg:

The term itself – "physical theatre" – denotes a hybrid character and is testimony to its double legacy in both avant-garde theatre and dance. It is precisely this double current of influences which needs to be taken into consideration in any attempt to delineate specific parameters of the new genre. […] the process of contextualizing physical theatre needs to take into consideration its location within both avant-garde theatre, particularly that production considered to be "body-focused", and also within the context of avant-garde dance and its particular parameters which set the body as the centralizing unit within the theatrical space.

(2007: 21)

Sánchez-Colberg traces its avant-garde dance lineage back to German Ausdrucktanz and its principle to "squeeze out from the inner landscape of the artist's body (and psyche) action that actualises the self in the world (the outer landscape)" (2004: 4), as exemplified in the avant-garde dance experimentations of Mary Wigman, the tanztheater of Pina Bausch, and the volatile aesthetic of DV8 Physical Theatre. She traces its avant-garde theatre lineage to the experimentations of Bertolt Brecht and the genre of the Theatre of the Absurd (2004: 5). While Sánchez-Colberg ignores the third lineage of mime as acknowledged by Chamberlain and Murray and Keefe, she comes closest to charting the genealogy of physical theatre as a hybridised genre, emerging at the interstices between avant-garde theatre and dance. This resonates with my own inter-disciplinary performance training and subsequent scholarship that is generated at the interstices between the disciplines of theatre and dance. Perhaps it is my own embodied hybridised understanding of the genre that draws me towards Sánchez-Colberg's approach when starting to delineate the genre in order to rectify the vagueness that surrounds it.

Sánchez-Colberg notes that physical theatre's hybrid identity between avant-garde theatre and avant-garde dance echoes the Artaudian philosophy of theatre making, where "the body is the centre of the *mise-en-scène*" (2007: 23). She attempts to clarify the nature of this body that occupies the third space between dance and theatre by reminding us that:

> whilst admitting to the significance of a "decoding" process of the body as a sign of discourse, it has also become significant to consider that the social body which is the focus of such structural analysis is also a spatial body, which, although subject to social discourse, also has its own "embodied" knowledge.
>
> (2007: 25)

I would like to extend Sánchez-Colberg's observation that this social/spatial body is not just a vessel through which the primary means of communication occurs. It is in fact the fundamental source and stimulus of interpersonal politics and sociopolitical relations with the world, and is inseparable from its embodied subject. Therefore, I would first like to suggest that this "body", who occupies the heart of avant-garde performance practices, needs to be reframed as an embodied subject. The reason I choose to use the term "embodied subject" over "body" is because while the former signals a lived reality that energises physical theatre processes and performance, the latter may suggest its historically passive manifestation in which the body is seen merely as a tool of communication, devoid of agency. Consequently I propose that in physical theatre, it is not the body that is at the centre of the *mise-en-scène*, but the embodied subject, whose live reality fuels the *mise-en-scène* and lends physical theatre its charge.

This conceptual shift from thinking about the body as a vessel of communication to understanding the body as an embodied subject needs brief contextualising in embodiment theory. Over centuries French philosopher René Descatres' concept of dualism has created the damaging split between the superior mind and the inferior body, generating philosophical debates that Elizabeth Grosz refers to as "the heirs of Cartesianism" (1994: 8). Grosz suggests that these heirs have identified three kinds of bodies of which the third is most pertinent to this discussion. This body is "commonly considered a signifying medium, a vehicle of expression" (Grosz, 1994: 9) that is fundamentally passive "through" which the subject experiences and communicates with the world. Dymphna Callery's claim that physical theatre is theatre that is created "through the body" (2000: 4), as though it were a mere medium of signification, perpetuates such passive notions of the body as distinct from its embodied subject. Dance scholar Sandra Horton Fraleigh counters such passive constructions of the body, by extending the embodiment debate through the notion of the "lived body" that "attempts to cut beneath the subject-object split" (1987: 4), and critiques the concept of the "body as an instrument, movement as the medium, and mind or soul as the mover or motivational source" (1987: 13). Physical theatre as a genre is therefore an art form that "is not merely about the body, but from the body" (Csordas, 2003: xi), and examines both the embodied subject's shaping of the world and the impact the world has on shaping such subjectivities. In this it evokes dance scholar Susan Leigh Foster's concept of "corporeality" as an examination of embodied subjectivities through their "bodily reality, not as natural or absolute given but as a tangible and substantial category of cultural experience" (1996: x). Physical Theatre recognises and draws on the embodied subject's "role in the production of narrative, in the construction of collectivity, in the articulation of the unconscious […]" (p. xiv). It emphasises the role of these subjects in their ability to "contour new relations between history and memory, the aesthetic and the political, the social and the individual" (Foster, 1996: xiv). It does not use the body as a mere vehicle of expression. Instead, it locates the embodied reality of its performers at the heart of its aesthetic. This shift from physical theatre being a "body-focused" aesthetic to an "embodied-subject-focused" aesthetic can be a fundamentally different way of engaging with the genre. In physical theatre then, the conventional theatrical boundaries between fiction and reality and character and self collapse as the performer's corporeality permeates the persona he/she represents on stage, and thereby becomes a heightened version of one's lived-self.

The importance of the "embodied-subject-focused" aesthetic in physical theatre, and the ownership of creative possibilities it can produce for a performer, is heightened further by the genre's genealogical alliance with democratic and non-hierarchical principles of collaborative devising methodologies. A 1970s critical and creative response to historical and hierarchical power-dynamics that govern conventional director–actor relationships, devising as a performance-making strategy, has "always been associated with the counter-cultural fringe" (Govan et al., 2007: 4). Historically, devising has been driven by the political agenda of collaboration within a creative collective that is non-hierarchised, giving birth to the idea of a creative performer who is free from the constraints of merely delivering the intentions of a script. In recent years, however, scholars have questioned this ideological position of devising. Alison Oddey suggests that in the "cultural climate of the early 1990s, the term 'devising' has less radical implications, placing greater emphasis on skill sharing, […] specific roles, increasing division of responsibilities […] and more hierarchical company structures" (1994: 9). In a similar vein Heddon and Milling have gone a step further to consider whether devising as a methodology was ever truly democratic and non-hierarchical, as it has always been very common for artistic directors and choreographers to lead ensembles in devising performances (2006: 5). They therefore observe how the role of a director or a choreographer can fundamentally "complicate the notion of non-hierarchical work or democratic participation" (2006: 5). This has led them to suggest that devising has acquired a "mythical status" in avant-garde performance-making processes in its idealistic "embodiment of death of the author" (Heddon and Milling, 2006: 4, 5). It is vital to question then that if an ensemble's shared vision is inspired, led and ultimately controlled by the vision of a director or choreographer, then to what extent can the work remain the product of non-hierarchical collaboration? The idea and practice of leading a devised process then becomes an anomaly that thwarts some of the fundamental principles of democracy and non-hierarchical creativity that devising once stood for.

It is common practice for contemporary physical theatre companies to claim their allegiances to collaborative devising methodologies while being led by the vision of an artistic director and/or a choreographer as in the case of Lloyd Newson for DV8 Physical Theatre, Akram Khan for Akram Khan Company, Charlotte Vincent for Vincent Dance Theatre, Scott Graham and Steven Hoggett for Frantic Assembly and of course Jasmin Vardimon for Jasmin Vardimon Company. However while these performance-makers all reject the idea of a single authorial voice, arguing repeatedly for the importance of multiple individual voices that are generated from experimentations by the ensemble, these voices are ultimately edited, shaped and honed by the artistic director to fit a holistic vision of the piece. Authorship in such physical theatre performances therefore becomes a complex and hybridised entity, shifting between the creative performers in the ensemble and all the other people in the hierarchy who interpret and contextualise their material through editing, filming, choreography, scriptwriting, design and dramaturgy. It is more useful perhaps then to consider the responsibility of authorship in such performances as a sliding scale between these different creative inputs: one end of the scale being ultimate directorial control and the other being a more open and collaborative approach for debate and discussion towards the making of the piece. The question of authorship becomes particularly potent in the physical theatre genre, which relies heavily on a corporeal crafting of signification through both athletic high-risk physicality and a language born from pedestrian, socialised gestures. Because of its close association with the discipline of dance, whose conventional use of the choreographer as one who creates phrases and imposes them onto performers' bodies to learn and deliver through repetition, the question that becomes vital to raise is: "Who authors the movement phrases and gestural language in physical theatre performances and how can authorship be maintained and owned when someone performs another person's phrases, particularly in reprised performances that are often not performed by an original cast?" If the question of authorship in the making of physical theatre can indeed be represented as a sliding scale, then it certainly calls into question the democratic principles of the once non-hierarchical spirit of collaborative devising methodologies, and in turn can complicate Roland Barthes's seminal concept of "the death of the author".

AUTHORSHIP AND *JUSTITIA*

In the spirit of established characteristics of devised performance texts, *Justitia* challenges "neat distinctions between the fictional and real, between secrets and lies, and between imagination and authenticity" (Govan et al., 2007: 56). Established frameworks of a logical and linear courtroom drama are abandoned for a more complex network of multiple narrative threads that go back and forth in time, as manifold versions of the night when Seth Marvell died are played out to the audience, authored and relayed from different perspectives. Some versions seem more convincing and plausible than others as we hear the defence lawyer Veronica Hunt deconstruct each possibility for the jury. It makes us question who actually authors the "truth". Does such a thing as "the whole truth and nothing but the truth" actually exist? Or, is it merely transformed through the different layers of fabrications generated by the different perspectives on offer and thus ultimately gets lost, or at the very least transmuted, in the name of a legal enquiry? This obscuring of fact and fiction in a legal trial can be compared to what Govan et al. describe as the complexity that accompanies watching a devised performance:

The process of shaping intimate thoughts, feelings and experiences for a witnessing audience inevitably fuses truth and fiction by recognising that the imagination is integral to the narrative of selfhood. The audience is frequently left wondering what is truthful and what is fictional; thus the question of the authenticity of narratives is raised.

(2007: 56)

The experience of watching a devised performance can thus be compared, on a micro-level, to the experience shared by jury members in a trial who have to witness multiple and often contrary statements presented from varied perspectives before reaching a verdict, thus contributing in their own way to the authoring of a version of "truth". In *Justitia* the different perspectives are obscured even further by hinting at the possibility that the seemingly distinct characters of the accused Mimi Cain, the defence lawyer Veronica Hunt and the stenographer Cassandra might just be slippery manifestations of each other. Interestingly it is no coincidence I am sure that the stenographer, who is responsible for the accurate recording of witnesses' statements at a trial, is called Cassandra, the Greek princess who had the ability to foresee facts about the future but whose predictions no one believed. While these three characters are visibly distinct through costumes, naturalistic behaviour and physical persona, in the language of stylised gestural movement work, they seem to morph into one another by copying/mirroring each other's gestures – thereby suggesting a certain malleability of their distinctness.

There are several instances when such morphing between the characters is witnessed but I want to focus briefly on the sequence where, through a flashback that contextualises Mimi's relationship with her husband Private Charlie Cain, Veronica tells the jury about his dominance over his wife. This relationship of stereotyped masculine dominance and feminine submission is played out through a powerful and disturbing duet through which Charlie controls and manipulates Mimi's actions. At one point Veronica stops talking as her body starts to take on the slightest hints of Mimi's submissive gestures. Veronica tries to shake off these movements, but they seem to gradually engulf her – until she is performing the same duet as Mimi and Charlie, as though with an invisible partner who controls her, like Charlie controls Mimi. This sequence reaches its climax when Veronica takes over Mimi in the duet with her husband, fully embodying Mimi's passivity. And a final slippage between the characters is suggested when Veronica and Charlie's duet is mirrored in the background in Cassandra and the deceased victim, Seth. The blurring of these characters in the trial exacerbates the idea that within a legal enquiry it remains unclear who actually authors whose story, and to what extent objectivity can be maintained by the so-called impartial roles of the defence lawyer and the stenographer, who simply wish to present the "truth". But whose truth?

In setting out to tell Mimi Cain's story, Vardimon leads her ensemble in an intelligent critique of the legal system, questioning its authoring and handling of "truth" by aligning multiple versions of "truths" against each other. Even at the end, when *Justitia* finally reveals the truth through Mimi's own confessional, Vardimon signals the precariousness of it by mediating her statement through a digital projection that translates Mimi's mother-tongue into English, transcribed by an anonymous typist. In the 2007 version Mimi spoke in Korean and in the 2012 version she spoke in Japanese, and both were translations from Lenkiewicz's English script. This mystery character appears intermittently through the piece, most memorably opening the performance through a choreographic evocation of orchestration and control and then towards the end as the translator and transcriber of Mimi's confession. When we first witness the anonymous typist in the opening sequence, her typing is rhythmic, mechanical, measured, considered and controlled, and even as her body breaks out into fluid lyrical phrases, her typing returns her to reality, echoed in the stenographer Cassandra's later proclamation "I type therefore I am – I am therefore I type". Towards the middle of the piece, in the solo that we witness from the anonymous typist, Cassandra's sentiments are expanded physically to almost spell out "I type therefore I orchestrate". And finally in the climax of the piece, her typed and translated transcription becomes the vital key to revealing the ultimate truth, Mimi's confession, to the audience. The audience are expected to trust her translation of this confession as "the truth" and this is emphasised by Mimi herself, completing her statement in English saying, "Is that what you wanted to hear? And what if I'm lying?" It is intriguing then that despite Mimi's ability to speak adequate English Vardimon choose to convey Mimi's confession in her first language. I interpret this artistic choice as strategy to demonstrate how the act of translation becomes a metaphor for the role of multiple authorships in legal enquiries, and also more subtly on the role of the director as a translator of multiple possibilities in the making of physical theatre.

This latter commentary is heightened in *Justitia* when the role of this anonymous typist is performed by Vardimon herself. Here the issues of authorship and orchestration shift from the specificities of *Justitia* to the generic processes of performance-making in the physical theatre genre, as Vardimon's strategic role as the anonymous typist may be seen as a crucial and honest suggestion of the very anomaly that characterises the challenge of leading a collaborative and non-hierarchical creative process. In physical theatre performances it is not uncommon to see the choreographer of a piece appear in the piece itself. But what makes Vardimon's appearance in *Justitia* interesting is its strategic placement vis-à-vis the other characters in the piece. The visual placement of Vardimon within the piece, particularly with regard to how she controls the telling of Mimi's story, becomes a commentary on Vardimon's authorship of the piece itself as the company's artistic director. The anonymous typist's crucial role as translator and transcriber of Mimi's confession lends the character tremendous power *vis-à-vis* communicating a fundamental piece of the jigsaw to the audience. The audience have no choice but to believe what the typist transcribes and as the jury, they base their judgement on mediated and translated second-hand knowledge that ultimately emanates from a source that is not the defendant and therefore does not come with any certainty of authenticity. In a similar way, Vardimon's strategic presence within a collaborative devised piece that she directs hints at dismantling the myth that circulates about the democratic multi-authorship of physical theatre performances, by signalling her orchestration and control over *Justitia*'s creative process.

In *Justitia* the crafting and performance of the courtroom drama scenario is presented as a network of multiple intersecting narratives that are ultimately controlled and orchestrated by the singular entity of the anonymous typist. I believe that this is a coded exploration of the innumerable individual creative possibilities generated by a physical theatre ensemble, whose contributions are shaped, edited and packaged by various different members of the creative team, under the ultimate orchestration of the company's artistic director and her vision. Just as the different narratives in *Justitia* tug in different directions and play on the tensions inherent in the different versions of the truth presented by the characters, the oxymoronic notion of directing a collaborative ensemble is filled with creative and philosophical tensions. However, contrary to negative associations attached to the notion of "tensions", I would like to propose that contemporary approaches to devising in physical theatre rest on looking for positive outcomes that can arise from such tensions. While creativity can be stifled within a conventional actor–director hierarchy, it is also true that one of the dangers of work created out of a non-hierarchical democratic process is that it can suffer from a lack of accessibility and objectivity. The contemporary practice of leading devised ensemble tries to rectify the challenges in both these oppositional models by searching for a balanced approach that aims to integrate the most productive features of both. As a constant inside-outsider to the creative process, an artistic director of a devised physical theatre piece therefore takes on the role of an internal dramaturge to maintain criticality and objectivity towards the material generated by the creator(s) through the creative process (Barton, 2005: 103). While nurturing and honing the creative possibilities and skills shared by her ensemble, she works to "question habit, to complicate unreflexive expediency, and to dig beneath the surface of unearned presumption" (Barton, 2005: 103) before permitting someone totally outside the creative process to undertake the same tasks. Vardimon's role as the anonymous typist in *Justitia* is symbolic perhaps of this inside-outsider role in the orchestration of the narratives that are told in *Justitia* and in the creative process of the piece itself. She thus complicates the idea of "the death of the author" by demonstrating that in the making of devised physical theatre, creative responsibility shifts (though not endlessly) between an ensemble and other members of a creative team, but is primarily shaped and controlled by the vision of the artistic director, who becomes the ultimate medium of translation for the audience. Like the multiple truths fabricated in a legal trial that ultimately give way to a singular version being accepted as "the" truth, the authorship of a physical theatre performance entails competing creative possibilities and individual narratives that are ultimately triumphed by "the" version that shapes and is shaped by the vision of the artistic director, who invariably orchestrates its final manifestation.

STAGE 1

Readers

*Our soul is a moving tableau which
we depict unceasingly;
we spend much time
trying to render it
faithfully,
but it exists
as a whole
and all at once.*

"Lettre sur les Sourds et Muets"
by Denis Diderot 1751

Conclusions

"A close friendship among the debris …"

Acting, Breath and Truth in Jasmin Vardimon's *Justitia*

Geoffrey Colman

Our soul is a moving tableau which we depict unceasingly; we spend much time trying to render it faithfully, but it exists as a whole and all at once.

"Lettre sur les Sourds et Muets"
by Denis Diderot 1751

In a publicity photograph, we see the haunting tableau of choreographer Jasmin Vardimon, her face in profile, sitting at a sparse table, staring intently at a sheet of white paper, lost, it seems, in the moment of writing. Bright beams of light encircle her tiny frame. The image is that of a dangerous, beautiful, sensual world, the world of Vardimon's *Justitia*.

"I'm going to share a little story with you …."

Not as an academic but as a collaborator, who worked with Vardimon and her company on the 2013 revival production, *Justitia*, as dramaturg and acting coach.

"Confession scene"

"I entered the rehearsal room, each day at 10.00, took lunch at 14.30.

I left the rehearsal room at 18.00 hours.

Vardimon and her dancers would warm-up from 10.00 until 11.15.

A physically gruelling preparation, conducted in near-silence.

Rehearsals were held on the original, carefully re-assembled set, which must have been taken out of storage, I think that I recognised it from the photographs.

Dancers were sometimes required to wear costumes from the original production too, and rehearsed with the original score, connected to the sound system by Vardimon's own iPod Classic, which was covered in a blue plastic case.

Maybe not blue. Green? I'm not sure.

The text, by playwright Rebecca Lenkiewicz, was not edited, cut or changed.
Vardimon's lips would sometimes form the letters of the words as they were spoken.

Those dancers playing Charlie, Seth, Veronica and Cassandra had been in the production before, and therefore knew their lines and moves.

I would also like to say, at this point, that the dancers were not coerced into any creative state, without their full knowledge, understanding and permission. I can also confirm that during all rehearsals Vardimon never left the room, but watched the dancers intently, often seated, and made extensive notes in Hebrew, and on recycled paper. She wrote with her right hand, in pen. I do not know what the notes said, for I do not speak Hebrew, but if I might add here – her company comprised many nationalities. The shared language was therefore kinaesthetic not linguistic. In rehearsals, Vardimon would often refer to her notes, pages and pages of them, and quietly correct the dancers with vocal instructions, or by physical demonstration. I do not know what she did with the pages once she had read out her notes. I wish I did. Once the notes were given, she would encourage, and question, often requiring movement phrases to be repeated many times. This never frustrated the dancers. I can vouch for this, and for the incredible focus that was required.

Nothing would distract. Nothing. No chit chat or small talk, no mobile phones, or strangers visiting the rehearsal room, no "just popping out", or "taking five". Sitting, sometimes beside her as I did, I swear that my account is …"

"Objection! There is nothing to substantiate this theory ..... "

" "

"Objection! There is nothing to substantiate this query ....."

"

"The set rotates, turning like the pages of a massive book ....."

Vardimon's work is perhaps best preserved within the living bodies, and muscle-memory of her performers. The first-hand witnesses of her aesthetic, who, as participants and creators, would come to the revival rehearsal each day, to question the durability of their own physical memory. Most but not all of them were in the original staging, all had worked with Vardimon before, and knew her work. Often, the physical and psychological answers they sought in order to revive the piece could only be found in the moment of performance itself. And so on the afternoon of the very first rehearsal, knowing this to be the case, smiling Vardimon calmly stated, "*OK let's run it*". The work was inside them – somewhere, in their knowledge-soaked bodies.

"All rise … "

From the initial moments of Charlie and Mimi's formal and exquisite courtship, to the "low-tech" informalities of their doomed relationship, re-wound as a drunken vaudeville, where two blokes, Seth and Charlie, drink from cans of beer, sit on the sofa and watch a match on TV, *Justitia* presents a crime of passion, forever spinning in the chaos of the sublime and mundane. Vardimon's original vision for this was large scale, monumental and technologically authoritative, often presenting the live and recorded digital sequences of its characters as "close-up" inner perspectives, simultaneously alongside sometimes near-static frozen moments, unceasingly turning upon a revolve, forming the essential evidence upon which the audience would experience what was true or false, or as Diderot suggests in "Lettre sur les Sourds et Muets", "as a whole and all at once".

"Shhh! Shhh! Alright Marvell, don't get carried away, remember what happened … "

Vardimon's revival rehearsals were not conducted as some sort of post-human experiment in remembering what had happened, but rather, the dancers were required to undertake very specific, intimate, physical orientations into the psychological worlds of character, where the reliability and account of an individual life becomes, in Vardimon's vision, a complex philosophical meta-theatrical fiction. For the revival, Vardimon required that her performers excavate memories of any previously exhaled breath, click or swoosh of sound, as a means of igniting a required move or thinking quality. The text, and the interior land-scape of its characters, was discussed at length, sometimes (it seemed to me) almost more than any discussion of movement. In the early stages, moves were often criticised by

Vardimon for looking too choreographed. New emotional and psychophysical triggers inevitably occurred during this collective reclamation process, but were then only permitted once the memory of the original idea or impulse had been fully understood. In this respect, Vardimon asked that I explore the overarching psychological thinking mechanism of the piece, noting with caution that any suggested changes of thought might result in not only a physical change of breath, but by default a modification of her original choreographic intention.

With every revolve of the rehearsal set, Lenkiewicz's text meant absolutely everything, and absolutely nothing. Character stories were inhabited and destroyed by the creeping but inevitable force and turn of 180 degrees. But if there are echoes of Lyotard's postmodernity here, Vardimon resisted the chaotic plane of "anything goes" in rehearsal, and challenged more fundamentally the conventional relationship between character and text, performer and personal; she disliked any sense of her dancers just putting physical moments together – without feeling, and encouraged me to demand of them, emotional, utterly inhabited worlds, thus challenging the historic distinctions between dance and theatre.

"Ok everyone. Let's give her some support …"

The week before rehearsals started at her Ashford studios in Kent, I was asked to visit the choreographer's home, having spent many hours prior to this watching video documentation, looking at photographs of the work and piecing together my own experiences of her company earlier in the year, at an intensive week-long preparatory workshop for the dancers who would be performing in the revival. Our meeting was arranged so that we might discuss, moment by moment, the entire piece. Not that the discussion was designed to somehow format my own response, or align it to Vardimon's immutable vision, but rather it was to explore the aesthetics of *Justitia*, and to imagine what it might become when revived. Vardimon's extraordinary identification, description and analysis of her own work was not limited to a recollection of steps or moves, but expounded a thesis on the necessary and essential qualities of story, and crucially, how breath was at the absolute core of any physically committed and connected "truth" in performance. Although a profusion of extended ideological and critical overviews have been published about her work, it was Vardimon's quietly spoken thoughts, her silence and stillness that was most resonant to me, and it was this quality that I always took into rehearsal.

"We have to look at the scientific facts …"

Vardimon demands that the performer is not initiated into a standardised way of seeing, or an agreed framework of understanding, and therefore does not require a predetermined, psycho-scientific way of looking at the world. In *Justitia*, characters are affected by their physical environment, and sometimes become it. Nothing is as it seems, Vardimon's non-linear stage discourses resemble the structure of dreams, and so as rehearsals progressed, and mindful of this non-hierarchy of narrative forms, performers worked to "wire-up" their own personal overarching sequence of thinking units, finding linear moments of order ("I think this, and then, I think that") inside chaotic molecules of thought ("I think this, and then, I become that"). This aspect of the rehearsal process was the most difficult and Vardimon would return to this time and time again. The glue that ultimately held these "chaotic molecules" together was described by Vardimon as "essences" or "qualities" of thought. The rehearsal studio became the collective site for what Derrida once described as "spectral" evidence, with ghostly moments, bodies, movement and sound being summoned and ex-amined. Vardimon's core aesthetic emanated from this place, thus challenging the notion that dancers do "this" or do "that", as though they inhabit their creative journey in a sort of cool, trance-like state of dumb passivity, hushed, in awe, and utterly compliant with whatever might be dreamt up.

"Hi Marvell. Hi Charlie …"

Justitia shares oblique formal points of contact with several of Jasmin Vardimon's works, notably *Park* (2005), *7734* (2010) and *Freedom* (2012), where a strong, at times near-lin-ear, physical narrative creates the enabling conditions for both movement and language. Words are not always spoken from a psychological centre, or a conception of character, but language exists as story, given physical agency not only through breath but also digital projection, amplification or just a basic need to speak. These points of contact are made all the more distinctive by the fact that her works are mostly colonised by dancers, who having performed with Vardimon over many years and enshrine the impossibly physical, almost un-performable artefacts of her repertoire, and crucially, in so doing, perpetuate Vardimon's methodology and aesthetic. But to suggest that she enters the rehearsal room with the inten-tion of creating vacuum-sealed, dance-theatre pieces is nonsense. Whilst her work has sometimes been generically identified as such, it is not exclusively (singularly) about dance, or about theatre – it inhabits both aspects freely and liminally, having detached itself from the more readily available orthodoxies of pure dance. Though complex, it exists without the presupposition or requirement of any determined or fixed response; the dancer is free to experience the emotional possibility of the work, as long as the essential qualities of each phrase are understood. In order to achieve this in rehearsal, Vardimon constructs imaginary as opposed to actual landscapes, so multifarious as to invoke the necessary violent, or sensual, demands of the piece. Her use of intertextual materials and eclectic range of music not only underscores and infuses the rehearsal room, but ultimately requires the performer to become the physical transmitter of their own sense of the story.

Justitia is such an exciting physical, visceral, at times lustily repellent, at times erotically charged, piece, where the degraded acts of passion-gone-wrong become exalted. In rehearsal, the dancers have to endure both the physical and emotional repetition of characters who, at each rotation of the set, think ever-increasingly of their own mortality or death. The sense of mortality pervades Vardimon's rehearsal room; bodies are frequently in states of profound exhaustion, dancers at once spinning slowly into a living room, courtroom, war zone or carnal bed, breath oxygenated by the present, but chased by the ever-revolving past. A love scene and nightmare in a single phrase.

As rehearsals progressed, Vardimon moved away from the process of mere reclamation to an overwhelming and detailed exploration of the performer's own need to surrender to the flat, bleached-out emptiness of the revolving, desperate set of possible stories, lost in space and time, forever frozen, forever on rewind. At times, the sheer weight and density of the process seemingly disallowed the performer's conscious ability to escape its oppressively real feeling. Remarkably, such abstraction and repetition cuts deep into the receptive performer, often without permission, when the performer is neither expecting nor wanting it. Vardimon's daily insistence on the agreed emotional qualities attached to a given moment laid dormant, virus-like, awaiting the right moment for physical placement.

Many of Vardimon's choreographic or physical phrases seem to almost restrict the dancer's body. In *Justitia*, she requires them to hang precariously from the full height of the moving stage set, or quickly jump in states of synchronised fear onto, or off of, a row of wooden chairs, or run at each other and then sit in absolute stillness. She requires her performers to dance inside their bodies as opposed to with their bodies, without removing the seductive, near-narcotic sense of freedom that Vardimon gives them. At such times, their minds and bodies must participate in a complex meditation on the very role and function of dance itself, and in so doing, their fundamental navigation of the performance process becomes obliquely objectified, and Vardimon's theatre becomes the mnemonic material upon which the performer surrenders his/her body to.

"Is that what you wanted to hear?"

Vardimon requires that her performers fully embrace the music and ambient sound played over the projected image, the fifteen counted steps to the right, the stillness, the waiting for a light source, or revolve, to complete its fade or turn. In such moments, there is essentially a dual rather than shared experience going on. The performer has to exist in a continual present – driving the discourse but not (in the moment) reflecting upon it, whereas the spectator is enabled to be free of the conditioned performed moment – unfettered by anything other than his/her own imaginative response to the piece. The dream-like, collapsing and dissolving narrative stasis of *Justitia* seems to tell of the dream world of its creators.

To perform in Vardimon's landscape is to perform in a kind of vacuum where thought, feeling and action are frozen in an ever-present, brutal place of endless, yearned-for possibility that obviates the need for a new performance alertness: "real" at its threshold and most porous. The major challenge in performing such work is to unleash a subjective accumulation of narratives that are complex "recognisable" responses to the text, alongside the need for the cool placement of oneself as revealed in movement. Vardimon's work, though impacting, essentially flattens the naturalist/realist dynamic. There is a contradiction here (one of many in her work), the reduction or annihilation of character and the scenographic, alongside the greater magnification of the theatrically "decorated" moment. This is seen in "smooth" collaboration of sound and light in an empty space, the musicalised language of a text that means nothing, the actor and technology, the tableaux vivant – the painful condition of the dream world, "as a whole and all at once".

"Animals protect their young. And that's how I feel more than ever before.
Animal.
Except animals don't feel guilt …"

Such work provokes the rehearsal context with the removed authority of poetry, where form is as important as content, and where Vardimon encourages her performers to enter the place of unknowing and unlearning.

Where the absence of "character" foregrounds body grammar and vocal usage, and the endless life and death of *Justitia*'s people reclaim the limitless sensual possibilities of the interior hidden moments of existence.

When assessing beauty, Diderot suggested that the judgements we make are done so from the senses, emotions and lastly intellect – and that the beauty response happens "all at once". Vardimon's theatre, like encountering great beauty, demands that the performer's senses, emotions and intellect engage "all at once", and as is clear when reading the chapters in this account of *Justitia*, a single moment is notoriously difficult to justify, let alone record or preserve, for the performance moment is but that – passing and complete – a living response to "liveness". The work of a choreographer is also measured in this extraordinary moment, but somehow in *Justitia* we become unaware of all of these contributing elements as the performance is actually elevated from the "all at once", and stands in our mind's eye, alone and in emotional close-up.

Perhaps the pleasure in witnessing this work is not about applying marks out of ten, but about one's personal connection to the beauty of the crafted truthful performance.

Once identified it enters the mind and stays adored.

"And what if I am lying?"

The set rotates, turning like the pages of a massive book ….

Bibliography

Anastasopoulou, S., (2009). 'The Chaos of Probabilities' in the Catalogue of the 15th Kalamata International Dance Festival. [online] Available at http://jasminvardimon.com/wp-content/uploads/2014/02/The-Chaos-of-Probabilities-2009.pdf [Accessed 20 February 2015]

Barton, B., (2005). Navigating Turbulence: The Dramaturg in Physical Theatre. *Theatre Topics*, 15(1). pp. 103–119.

Callery, D., (2001). *Through the Body: A Practical Guide to Physical Theatre*. London: Nick Hern.

Chamberlain, F., (2007). Gesturing Towards Post-Physical Performance. In: J. Keefe and S. Murray, eds. *Physical Theatres: A Critical Reader*. Abingdon: Routledge. pp. 117–122.

Csordas, T. J., (2003). Preface. In: T. J. Csrdas, ed. *Embodiment and Experience: The Existential Ground of Culture and Self*. Cambridge: Cambridge University Press. p. xi.

Cullmann, O., (1964). *Christ and Time: The Primitive Christian Conception of Time and History*. Louisville, KY: Westminster John Knox Press.

Damasio, A., (2006 Revised [1994]). *Descartes Error*. London: Vintage Books.

Derrida, J. and Blanchot, M., (2000). *The Instant of My Death and Demeure: Fiction and Testimony* (trans. Elizabeth Rottenberg). Redwood City: Stanford University Press.

Foster, S. L., (1996). Introduction. In: S. L. Foster, ed. *Corporealities: Dancing Knowledge Culture and Power*. London: Routledge. pp. i–xvii.

Fukuyama, F., (1992). *The End of History and the Last Man*. New York: Free Press.

Fraleigh, S. H., (1987). *Dance and the Lived Body: A Descriptive Aesthetics*. Pittsburgh: University of Pittsburgh Press.

Freud, S., (2006). Remembering, Repeating, and Working Through. In: A. Phillips, ed. *The Penguin Freud Reader*. London: Penguin.

Govan, E., Nicholson, H. and Normington, K., (2007). *Making a Performance: Devising Histories and Contemporary Practices*. Abingdon: Routledge.

Grosz, E., (1994). *Volatile Bodies: Towards a Corporeal Feminism*. Bloomington: Indiana University Press.

Heddon, D. and Milling, J., (2006). *Devising Performance: A Critical History*. Basingstoke: Palgrave Macmillan.

Kassin, S. M. and Neumann, K., (1997). On the Power of Confession: An Experimental Test of the Fundamental Difference Hypothesis. *Law and Human Behaviour*, 21(5).

Kenney, M., (2009). An Examination of Critical Approaches to Interdisciplinary Dance Performance. *Research in Dance Education*, 10(1). pp. 63–74.

Lansdale, J., (2004). Ancestral and Authorial Voices in Lloyd Newson and DV8's Strange Fish. *New Theatre Quarterly*, 20(2). pp. 117–126.

Lepecki, A., (1997). As If Dance Were Visible. *Performance Research*, 1(3). pp. 71–76.

Murray, S. and Keefe, J., (2007). *Physical Theatres: A Critical Introduction*. Abingdon: Routledge.

Oddey, A., (1994). *Devising Theatre: A Practical and Theoretical Handbook*. London: Routledge.

Phelan, P., (2001). *Unmarked: The Politics of Performance*. London: Routledge.

Reynolds, D., Reason, M., Grosbas, M., Pollick, F. E., Kuppuswamy, A., et al. (2011). Watching Dance: Kinaesthetic Empathy. [online] Available at http://www.watchindance. org/index.php [Accessed 20 February 2015]

Roy, S., (2003). [No title]. [online] Available at http://jasminvardimon.com/wp-content/ uploads/2014/02/Londondance.com_2003.pdf [Accessed 20 February 2015]

Roy, S., (2008) Jasmin Vardimon Company. *Guardian* 24 November. [online] Available at http://www.theguardian.com/stage/2008/nov/24/review-jasmin-vardimon-company-dance [Accessed 20 February 2015]

Sacks, O., (1986 [1985]). *The Man Who Mistook His Wife for a Hat.* London: Picador.

Sánchez-Colberg, A., (2004). *An(n)a Annotated: A Critical Journey.* Theatre enCorps Website. [online] Available at www.theatree corps.com/resources/Anna%20Annotated.pdf [Accessed 5 March 2011]

Sánchez-Colberg, A., (2007). Altered States and Subliminal Spaces: Charting the Road Towards a Physical Theatre. In: J. Keefe and S. Murray, eds. *Physical Theatres: A Critical Reader.* Abingdon: Routledge. pp. 21–25.

Schneewind, P., (1992). Autonomy Obligation and Virtue: An Overview of Kant's Moral Philosophy. In: P. Guyer, ed. *The Cambridge Companion to Kant.* Cambridge: Cambridge University Press. pp. 309–341.

Schneider, R., (2011). *Performing Remains: Art and War in Times of Theatrical Re-enactment.* London: Routledge.

Summers, R. S., (1999). Substantial Truth in Juridical Fact-Finding: Their Justified Divergences in Some Particular Cases. *Law and Philosophy*, 18(5).

Taylor, D., (1997). Disappearing Acts: Spectacles of Gender and Nationalism in Argentina's "Dirty War". Durham, NC: Duke University Press.

Turner, M., (2005). Hospital Lullaby. *Animated Magazine*, Summer. [online] Available at http://www.communitydance.org.uk/DB/animated-library/hospital-lullaby.html?ed=14057 [Accessed 20 February 2015]

Vardimon, J., (2012). Jasmin Vardimon Company. [online] Available at http://www.jasminvardimon.com/about.html [Accessed 13 August 2012]

MULTIMEDIA SOURCES

Justitia: A Gripping Courtroom Dance Drama by Jasmin Vardimon Company. 2007 [DVD].

Notes on Contributors

PAUL BRILL is an experienced Solicitor Advocate who has regular conduct of trials in the Crown Courts and Magistrates Courts.

GEOFFREY COLEMAN is Head of Acting at Royal Central School of Speech and Drama. He is regularly invited to give masterclasses and workshops both in the UK (Old Vic Theatre, Young Vic Theatre, Soho Theatre, Globe Theatre) and abroad (Czech Republic, Finland, Germany, Ireland, Prague, Spain). Geoffrey is currently Artistic Director of Festival 10 at the Theatre Royal Haymarket and one of the Haymarket's 'associate masters'. His freelance directing career has combined work in opera and theatre and in recent years has focused on the postdramatic and new writing. As a director and professional acting coach he has worked with playwrights and actors from various performance contexts ranging from dramaturgs/writers at the National Theatre of Finland and Institut del Teatre Barcelona, to Miramax, Lenny Henry, and international fusion collective Transglobal Underground award-winning singer Natasha Atlas. Increasingly consulted by the media, Geoffrey has broadcast and written on a range of performance-related issues. Recent onscreen includes Britain's Next Top Model, Skillicious (ITV) etc. Interviews and articles include Times Higher Education, The Independent, The Times, The Stage, Theatre Research International, BBC and ITV.

SYLWIA DOBKOWSKA is a Principal of Santa Monica International School in Japan. She completed her BA, MA and PhD studies in the UK. Originally from Poland, Sylwia has also worked as a Project Manager for the European Commission. Her enthusiasm for education developed through her experience as an academic researcher, editor and a designer. She researches visual representations of language in the form of text and visual art, merging academic theory and design practice.

FELIX ENSSLIN is Professor of Aesthetics and Art Education at the Academy of Fine Arts in Stuttgart. He is a director, dramaturg and curator and works with a focus on contemporary aesthetic and philosophical discourses and the psychoanalytic theory of culture.

CHRISTINE HARMAR-BROWN has combined work as a writer and freelance director with working in television as script editor on Casualty and then as Head of Development with La Plante Productions. Theatre credits include 15 Minutes developed with the Royal National Theatre Studio, Blessings: Old Red Lion, Cinderella: De La Warr Pavilion, Roofless, Carol and The Incident for dAb Arts, Class and Corruption and adaptations of five Shakespeare plays for The Mercatoria Company. In addition to her writing and directing work, Christine is a Co-Director of B&R Productions. Originally set up to produce New Writing and revivals of contemporary classics, B&R Productions also provide mentoring and creative consultancy services and in 2009 launched The School Creative Centre in Rye, an award winning multi-disciplinary studio facility for over 30 artists with gallery space, print room, theatre and workshop.

PAUL JOHNSON is Associate Dean and Head of the School of Performing Arts at the University of Wolverhampton. His current role is to lead the development of the Faculty's academic portfolio, including the introduction of new courses, and to manages the Faculty's quality enhancement, including QAA and Periodic Review processes. He has responsibility for developing and managing the Faculty's international and UK partnerships, which involve students studying across the world. His areas of research interest are in interdisciplinary approaches to performance, such as science and philosophy; applied drama, in particular museum and heritage theatre; and experimental performance in Europe and the USA. He is an active researcher, is currently supervising a number of PhD students, and has authored and edited books, articles and chapters on a variety of aspects of theatre and performance, presenting his work at academic conferences around the world.

EMILY KASRIEL develops thought leadership and strategic partnerships for the BBC World Service Group (BBC World Service radio, BBC World News TV and BBC.com), which reaches over a quarter of a billion people every week. She is also an Associate Fellow at the Skoll Centre for Social Entrepreneurship at the University of Oxford. Emily previously served as an award-winning producer, broadcaster and editor at the BBC. She developed, edited and occasionally presented The Forum, the flagship weekly discussion show on the BBC World Service, which brings together some of the world's most eminent minds from different disciplines to discuss ideas. Emily also ran the Arts and Religion departments of the BBC World Service, and has reported and produced for the BBC across five continents. She has also published long form articles exploring ideas for a number of publications including The Guardian, The Telegraph and the Financial Times, and regularly chairs panels and discussions at conferences and events. Emily also acts as a BBC Executive Coach, sits on the board of the charitable Wingate Foundation, and serves on the advisory board of Spark Inside, an NGO which transforms the lives of young people who have offended.

ROYONA MITRA is a Senior Lecturer in Theatre in the Department of Arts and Humanities at Brunel University London where she teaches physical theatre, intercultural performance and critical theory. Her interdisciplinary research between dance and theatre studies addresses intersectionalities between bodies, cultures and identities. She is the author of *Akram Khan: Dancing New Interculturalism* (Palgrave, 2015), the first book-length project to examine the works of this seminal British-Asian artist, and has also published in *Dance Research Journal*, *Feminist Review* and *Women & Performance* and contributed to edited anthologies on dance, identity and culture. Royona is currently developing a research project entitled 'Queering Dance / Theatre: Resistive Choreographies in Physical Theatre'.

NOAM SEGAL is an independent curator based in Tel Aviv. She holds a BA in Philosophy and Politics, MA in Hermeneutics and is currently a PhD candidate at Bar Ilan University. Her research deals with Installation Art as a Social Agent: Strategies of Constructing Social and Communal Positions. She successfully founded and curated Rothschild 69 non profit art space, based in Tel Aviv. She was part of the founding team of *Programma*, a quarterly art magazine in which she also acted as a content editor. Segal curated exhibitions at the Tel Aviv Museum of Art, Herzliya Museum of Contemporary Art, Petach Tikva Museum, Chicago Museum of Contemporary Photography, Velan Center for Contemporary Art in Turin, Ein Harod museum of Art, Performa 13' in NYC and more. Segal organised and curated several symposiums among them "Bedaya" in Arabic, at Rothschild 69, "Hearat Shulaim" in Petah Tikva Museum, Sderot Conference of the Israeli society, collaborative video symposium with the Pompidou center and more. She has published texts in various local and international magazines, and exhibition catalogues. She teaches in Bezalel MFA program, MA program for curatorial studies, and the BFA program in photography. She also thought at Hamidrasha school of art MA program for art education and Minshar school of Art. Segal received several grants by IKT association, the French Institute, and more and participated in various residency programs as BAR in Barcelona and KW young curators program as part of Berlin Biannale.

NINA STEIGER develops stories and performances with theatre-makers – companies, artists and agencies - across the UK. Recent projects include collaborations with Bryony Kimmings, Fuel and Inua Ellams, RashDash, Kim Noble, Theatre Uncut, High Tide and Out of Joint Theatre. As Associate Director at Soho Theatre, she commissions and develops new work; before this, she worked as a writer and director in New York. Nina also serves as a consultant, working with artists as well as organisations and brands on narrative development, audience engagement, strategy and creative direction and in particular, the role of great stories in the creative and commercial worlds. She fulfills regular teaching commitments with some of London and the UK's leading writing programmes and courses. She is passionate about digital media and new story platforms with a particular interest in crafting unique experiences for audiences using interactivity, game design, new technologies and transmedia narratives. Nina is a Fellow of the Clore Leadership Programme.

AMANDA STUART FISHER is a Reader in Contemporary Theatres and Performance at Royal Central School of Speech and Drama London where she teaches in areas such as applied theatre and writing for performance. Her research explores the dramaturgical challenges of writing plays about real events of trauma and testimonial and verbatim theatre. More recently she has begun a collaborative research project with applied theatre and social work researchers, which examines how testimony and performance can be used within social work training contexts to support social workers when working with families affected by child sexual abuse. Her work has been published in journals such as *TDR*, *Performance Research*, *Studies in Theatre and Performance* and *RiDE*. Her verbatim play *From The Mouths of Mothers* (2013), is published by Aurora books.

LIBBY WORTH is a Senior Lecturer in Theatre Practice and Director of MA Programmes at Royal Holloway, University of London. She is a movement practitioner trained in the Feldenkrais Method and Anna Halprin Life/Art dance processes. Recent performances include - *Step Feather Stitch* (2012) - devised and performed with visual artist Julie Brixey-Williams and documented in *Choreographic Practices* (2012). She is currently guest editor of *Theatre Dance and Performance Training* journal for the special issue on Moshe Feldenkrais (July 2015) and is writing a book with Jasmin Vardimon on her work (Routledge, due 2016). Her publications include co-editing with Richard Cave, *Ninette de Valois: Adventurous Traditionalist* (Dance Books, 2012), chapters on Mabel Todd in *Dancing Naturally: Nature, Neo-Classicism and Modernity in Early Twentieth-Century Dance* (Palgrave Macmillan, 2011), Caryl Churchill and Ian Spink for Cambridge University Press (2009) and a book, *Anna Halprin*, co-written with Helen Poynor (Routledge, 2004).